# *Bowing Before God....*

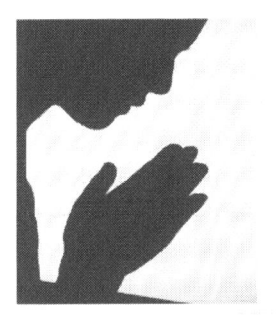

*A Woman's Devotional*

Written by
## Joan M. Koss
Co-authored by Teila Tankersley

© 2011 by Joan M. Koss
ISBN-13: 978-1463619480
ISBN-10: 1463619480
All rights reserved

## TABLE OF CONTENTS

**Chapter**                                                                                          **Page**

*Introduction..................................................................................................6*
*Dedication....................................................................................................8*
*Prelude.......................................................................................................10*
*Day One – Approaching "The Throne of Grace."—Hebrews 4:16................12*
*Day Two - The Sharpened Axe Gets the Work Done......................................14*
*Day Three - He Who Has No Sin; Cast the First Stone...................................16*
*Day Four - Cleaning Out the Cobwebs From Our Life....................................18*
*Day Five - Anxiety, Fear, and Abandonment..................................................20*
*Day Six - In Times of Trouble........................................................................23*
*Day Seven - Plea Bargaining..........................................................................25*
*Day Eight - Gott Ist Die Liebe........................................................................27*
*Day Nine - My Dad........................................................................................30*
*Day Ten - The Dreamer..................................................................................32*
*Day Eleven - The Ultimate Weight Loss........................................................35*
*Day Twelve - The Road to Damascus............................................................38*
*Day Thirteen - Pacing the Hospital Floor Can be One of the ..........................*
*Longest Days of Your Life.............................................................................40*
*Day Fourteen - The Lesson............................................................................42*
*Day Fifteen - Unconditional Love and Joy....................................................44*
*Day Sixteen - My Youngest Daughter...........................................................46*
*Day Seventeen - Seeking the Perfect World..................................................48*
*Day Eighteen - Anticipation and Insecurity..................................................49*
*Day Nineteen - My First Born........................................................................51*
*Day Twenty - "Be Still and Know that I Am God".........................................53*
*Day Twenty-One - Brazil...............................................................................55*
*Day Twenty-Two - The Heart Beat that Changes Everything.......................58*
*Day Twenty-Three - Sitcom...........................................................................60*
*Day Twenty-Four - Parenting and Patience..................................................69*
*Day Twenty-Five - Living Water...................................................................72*
*Day Twenty-Six - Peer Pressure....................................................................75*
*Day Twenty-Seven - My Sister, Lil................................................................80*
*Day Twenty-Nine - Golf.................................................................................82*
*Day Thirty - What's In a Name......................................................................85*
*Day Thirty-One - Gone Fishing.....................................................................89*
*Day Thirty-Two - The Master Weaver...........................................................93*
*Day Thirty-Three - Feelings of Loneliness....................................................96*
*Day Thirty-Four - Homelessness.................................................................100*
*Day Thirty-Five - Women of Strength, Women of Valor.............................105*
*Day Thirty-Six - The Tale of Two Women..................................................110*
*Day Thirty-Seven - The Wall I Built Brick by Brick...................................116*
*Day Thirty-Eight - Our Miracle Baby..........................................................119*
*Day Thirty-Nine - Respect............................................................................122*
*Day Forty – The Number 40........................................................................124*

. . . . . . . . .

# Introduction

Joan's life was pretty uneventful growing up, but she eventually discovered that no one is exempt from heartache and pain.

Joan and her family lived a middle class lifestyle in Colorado Springs, Colorado, and by all appearances it looked as though everything was all right. But in reality, the ground beneath her was slowly breaking away.

In the late 1970's, she experienced sorrow and frustration as her oldest daughter, who had just won the title of "District Ideal Miss", began hanging out with the wrong crowd. In one incident her daughter was shot and in another, she was held at gunpoint but eventually released. These unfortunate experiences stirred the family to uproot and move to a nearby town, where they thought they could start all over.

Shortly after the move, Joan's youngest daughter was hospitalized after a bomb exploded near the racetrack where she was racing quarter midget cars. It was a tragedy that nearly took her daughter's life, sending her off in an ambulance directly to surgery. Her daughter endured years of plastic surgery to repair the damage.

Joan watched as her picture perfect life disintegrated further. She helplessly stood by as her only son chose a life of drugs and alcohol, and was eventually sentenced to prison for manslaughter.

That wasn't the end. Just when she didn't think she could take any more, her marriage crumbled and fell apart. Devastated, Joan attempted suicide. Miraculously, she was *able to pull herself up through prayer, and discovered a life worth living.*

*Joan says, "I'm an ordinary woman who defied the odds, counted the cost, and took up the cross of Christ to overcome difficult and trying times that almost destroyed me. But, it wasn't until I dropped to my knees in the midst of my deepest despair and approached the throne of God, that I discovered a new hope, meaning, and purpose in life. God restored the years the cancer worm and the locust had taken away, and He can do it for you."*

*Are you carrying the weight of your past or present hurts, anxiety, anger, guilt, greed? Maybe it's time you approached the throne of God and bowed before the Living God. This 40-day devotional is written from the heart of Joan M. Koss. It's a book filled with inspiration, encouragement and promises from the Father up above.*

## *Dedication*

***In memory of my mother:*** *Clara, who taught me all about the Love of Jesus.*

***My oldest daughter:*** *Teila for all the hard work she has put into this book.*

***My son:*** *Darin for giving me my spiritual guidance.*

***My youngest daughter:*** *Tona for my strength. I'm blessed to have children that are behind me in everything I do and encouraging me every step of the way.*

***To my good friend, Nancy:*** *Thank you so much for helping to edit this book. Your friendship is priceless.*

***To my niece, Marvie:*** *Thank you for putting the final touches on this book. I appreciate you.*

*A special thanks goes to my grandchildren for sharing their ideas and talents in helping put together this devotional.*

## *Prelude*

*Our individual walk with God is a personal one, yet we often learn from one another. This devotional is based upon my personal experiences and relationship with God. In the pages of my book, I open up, expressing my deepest and inner most feelings and thoughts. I expose my weakness and my desperation, all in an effort to encourage you and to strengthen you. If God could save a wretch like me, and if I can have such an amazing relationship with the King of Kings and the Lord of Lords, so can you.*

*I pray my experiences and my journey inspire you to draw closer to Christ, in Jesus name. Amen.*

*-Joan M. Koss*

## *Day One*
*Approaching "The Throne of Grace."—
Hebrews 4:16*

*For too long, I had skipped this step in my relationship with the Lord. Oh, I prayed, but my prayers were more like a "Honey Do List". I'd pray, "God bless my children today, help me get through the day, help the finances flow in and make this world a better place. Amen."*

*In essence, I was not grasping who God really was. I had the head knowledge that He was Master, Savior, Jesus, the lamp onto my feet, but, my flesh and my heart were not getting it. I guess you could say I was taking God for granted. I had forgotten what a privilege and honor it is to know such royalty.*

*It's no wonder that my life was falling apart. I was in need of the anointing of God that can only be found at the throne of Grace.*

*The Bible instructs us to "Therefore come boldly unto the throne of grace that we may obtain mercy, and find grace to help in time of need. I've since learned that there is no other peace that can come close to the peace that I feel when I humbly approach the throne and just bask in his presence.*

*True prayer is not simply an utterance of word. It is in knowing that He is there and taking the time to acknowledge who He really is.*

*Our Savior, Our King, and Our Lord.*

## Day Two
## *The Sharpened Axe Gets the Work Done*

*I grew up on a farm, and I learned the importance of rising early and what it means to put in a good day's work. Anything to make the day easier and productive is profitable.*

*The New Century Version translates Ecclesiastes 10:10, "A dull ax means harder work. Being wise will make it easier." That seems obvious enough. Wisdom is to sharpen the axe so that the work can be completed faster and with less effort. This truth extends into the use of one's talents and abilities in life. To get better results, sharpen the axe. To sharpen the axe, get wisdom.*

*If you don't think you have time in the morning to pray and meditate, then you are missing out.*

Begin your day one on one with the Lord, seeking His wisdom for your life. *I've learned that it's much easier to wake up asking God what he has in store for me, and then seek His wisdom.*

*It's not about asking Him for things, it's more about bowing before the most-high God with sincerity and in respect, seeking His wisdom in "our" circumstances.*

*At a church retreat that I attended one year, the guest speaker's message was about asking God to show us His face, not His hands.*

*It dawned on me. The wisdom of God is what solves problems and sets the plans for the future. The very definition of wisdom is the application of knowledge. At that moment, I knew that's what I wanted. I wanted to see what God's plan was for me.*

*God has great plans for us.*

*Too often, we don't seem to realize that He is our Heavenly Father, and He does know what is best for us, He is able to see our lives from a fresh perspective. His desire for us is to be blessed.*

*Trusting God in hard times becomes uncomplicated and more manageable when we realize that God is on our side.*

*Begin your day one on one with the Lord, seeking his wisdom for your life.*

## *Day Three*
*He Who Has No Sin; Cast the First Stone.*

*I had grown up in a strict Christian home, so I felt that I had it more together than most. That couldn't have been further from the truth.*

*As a newly married young woman, and as a parent of small children, I had a hidden sin that not too many people knew about. My sin was "PRIDE and a Holier than thou attitude."*

*Somewhere deep inside, I just truly believed that my mother's faith is what would protect me. But we all know that our mothers are merely our teachers and mentors. It would be up to me to create my own relationship with God.*

*It wasn't until I was a young mother that I realized the limitations of a mother's love. In spite of my mother's prayers, my sins were keeping me from all that God had for me.*

*All have sinned and come short of the Glory of God.
Romans 3:23 KJV*

*My sin was pride. In the Bible, pride is portrayed as a necklace, a crown, and fruit. The Bible also says it persecutes, testifies, deceives, and brings low.*

*It is often seen as the first sin.*

*It is the sin which caused the devil to fall from his privileged position as an angel of light. The devil then used the same sin to tempt Adam and Eve away from their fellowship with Almighty God. Satan still tempts us today with the sin of pride.*

*God hates pride. (Prov 8:13)KJV*

*I had to lay my sin down at the foot of the cross. It's not that God expects perfection, it's just that these sins are our stumbling blocks, and we need to let them go. God is just to forgive us of our sins.*

*1 John 1:9 KJV If we confess our sins, He is faithful and just to forgive us our sins, and to cleanse us from all unrighteousness.*

## *Day Four*
## *Cleaning Out the Cobwebs from Our Life*

*Growing up, my mother was a stickler about having a clean house. Twice a year, we'd thoroughly clean house from top to bottom. Scrubbing baseboards and cleaning out closets was done whether they needed to be washed and cleaned or not.*

*It wasn't always fun, but when it was all finished, there was nothing like the feeling of having a freshly cleaned house, and seeing the reflection and the beauty of those crystal clear window panes. Every Saturday, the laundry was done with an old wringer type washing machine, and the sheets hung out on the line to dry. At the end of a long day, there was nothing so fresh and clean smelling as those sheets on the bed and the comforting feeling of climbing into that cozy bed after our Saturday night bath.*

*In my walk with Christ, it is also just as important to do some house cleaning. Every now and then we need to clean out all the strife in our life, and get rid of all the negativity.*

*Those spiders are busy spinning our secrets, our worries and our sins into cobwebs. These cobwebs will destroy our life, our peace, and even our health unless we deal with them. The Bible says to confess our sins. When your spiritual closets are clean, the heaviness from hidden sin will lift.*

*Sometimes we just need a deep cleaning in our hearts and lives to have a concentrated effort to seek out the areas of our lives that we have neglected.*

*In the presence of God, He sheds new light. This new light exposes the cobwebs in your life.*

Isaiah 59:6 KJV
Their webs shall not become garments; neither shall they cover themselves with their works: their works [are] works of iniquity, and the act of violence [is] in their hands.

*Psalm 51:10 KJV*
*Create in me a clean heart, O God; and renew a right spirit within me.*

*Hebrews 10:22 KJV*
*Let us draw near with a true heart in full assurance of faith, having our hearts sprinkled from an evil conscience, and our bodies washed with pure water.*

## *Day Five*
## *Anxiety, Fear, and Abandonment*

*The world was too much for me. My mind leaped from problem to problem to problem, entangling my thoughts in anxiety knots.*

*I now was facing divorce among everything else that was happening in our family.*

*Even though God yearned to help me, He would not violate my freedom that He created me with. You see, God will not come in unless invited. He will not move in our circumstances unless asked. He has given us independence and freedom. In our time of need, He stands close by, waiting for us to ask Him for direction and for comfort.*

*As Christ waited patiently by my side, He waited for me to draw nigh unto him. He held the wisdom, the peace, and the clarity that I needed.*

*I've often wondered why He doesn't just bulldoze the door down in our time of need and shout, "Hey you need me, I'm here to offer you comfort." However, I have come to realize in my own life, that doesn't usually work. How many times has someone offered us advice and direction in the midst of our crises and yet we refuse to listen, thinking we have a better plan? I know, I've been guilty of that.*

*Until we have exhausted all our own ideas, and until we are ready to seek God's wisdom, and His guidance and direction falls on deaf ears.*

*In the meantime, He stands patiently by, waiting for us to call upon His name. He holds the answers and wants nothing more than to be there for us.*

*While sitting in that mental hospital locked up, I was at my wit's end. I had no one else to turn to except for the Lord. That's when I cried out to God, "Where are you God? Do you not see that I'm hurting? Do you even care if I hurt?"*

*At that moment, I heard this small, still voice that said, "I haven't left you. I'm right here with you."*

*When I turned from my problems to His Presence, my load immediately got lighter. Although my circumstances hadn't changed, my burdens didn't feel so overwhelming.*

*It was then that things started changing in my life, and my mind was being set free.*

*Hebrews 13:5b KJV*
*"I will never leave thee, nor forsake thee."*

*Philippians 4:6, 7 KJB*
*Be careful for nothing; but in everything by prayer and supplication with thanksgiving let your requests be made known unto God.*

*(7)And the peace of God, which passeth all understanding, shall keep your hearts and minds through Christ Jesus.*

*I Peter 5: 7 KJV*
*Casting all your care upon him; for He careth for you.*

*Romans 8:28 KJV*
*And we know that all things work together for good to them that love God, to them who are the called according to his purpose.*

*John 16:33 KJV*
*These things I have spoken unto you, that in me ye might have peace. In the world ye shall have tribulation: but be of good cheer; I have overcome the world.*

*Isaiah 41:13 KJV tells us "For I am the Lord, thy God, will hold thy right hand, saying unto thee, Fear not; I will help thee."*

# ***Day Six***
## *In Times of Trouble*

*In the mid 80's my teenage daughter was kidnapped. I felt so helpless. It was hard to focus on trusting God. Yet, who else did I have to turn to?*

*I was a nervous wreck. My mind was spinning round and round going nowhere, accomplishing nothing.*

*I cried out to God. I exhausted my energy trying to figure out what I should do. I was worried sick.*

*Although I didn't know where my daughter was and had no idea if I'd ever see her again, I clung to the fact that I knew God knew where she was, and God wouldn't let her out of his sight.*

*God was involved in each and every moment of her life, and of my life, and in your life. He has mapped out every inch of our journey.*

*I had no choice but to trust in God. I had depleted all that I knew to do. I had to trust God in my moment of panic.*

*Unfortunately, we do live in a corrupt world. Isn't it good to know that even when we do not have the strength or the answers, that we can reach out for the hand of God!*

*I had no other choice, but to stay conscious of the Lord. I had to trust that no matter what happened that God was still on the throne.*

*I was doing all I could and now I had to allow the Holy Spirit to calm my fears, to guide my steps and to be with my daughter.*

*Trusting God in hard times is not always easy.*

*Psalms 119: 132-135 KJV*
*Look thou upon me, and be merciful unto me, as thou usest to do unto those that love thy name. (133)Order my steps in thy word; and let not any iniquity have dominion over me. (134)Deliver me from the oppression of man; so will I keep thy precepts. (135)Make thy face to shine upon thy servant; and teach me thy statutes.*

*(God is always near - photo taken by Shannon Tankersley)*

## *Day Seven*
## *Plea Bargaining*

*When my oldest was kidnapped and held at gunpoint, the court process was all new to me. I remember thinking to myself, "Why do they even offer plea bargains why not just hang them all?"*

*My first experience with "pardoning" left me feeling frustrated. It was something that just didn't make sense to me.*

*As I sat in the courtroom listening to the judge grant my daughter's kidnapper a plea bargain, my heart stopped.*

*What I've come to realize is that right or wrong, sometimes we all plea bargain with God at one time or another.*

*We serve a "just" God, but He is also a God of second chances, and often times even third or fourth chances.*

*—verb (used with object)
To deal with or achieve by plea bargaining: to plea-bargain a reduced sentence.*

*In the ultimate plea bargain of human history, Jesus, himself, went willingly to the cross on our behalf.*

*This is what Jesus refers to as the "new covenant". "For this is my blood of the new covenant, which is shed for many for the remission of sins." (Matthew 26:28)KJV*

*We have all sinned and come short of the glory of God but Jesus has made a new covenant or a plea bargain on our behalf. He died for our sins that we might have life.*

*On Judgment Day, Jesus will be there. When it comes our turn to stand before God, Jesus will stand on our behalf, once again, and say that when we accepted Christ as our Savior, and ask for His forgiveness, and turned from our sin, that He washed us white as snow with the blood that He shed on Calvary.*

*There will come a day that we will stand before the throne on Judgment Day, and all our sins will be revealed. This will not be a time for excuses. Instead we will either pay the ultimate price for our sin, or we will be pardoned because we made that decision when we were still alive to kneel before the throne and ask for a pardon.*

Meiningen Gesangbuch, 1693

*Gott ist die Lie-be, Lasst mich er-loes-en; Gott ist die Lie-be, Er liebt auch mich.*

*Drum sag ich noch ein-mal: Gott ist die Lie-be, Gott ist die Lie-be, Er liebt auch mich.*

## *Day Eight*
## *GOTT IST DIE LIEBE*

*Something that my mother passed down to me were Christian songs. She raised me on them, and she taught my children these precious melodies.*

*God wants us to trust him and not be afraid. In Isaiah, He tells us that He is our Strength and Song.*

*Yes, those lyrics were engrained in my heart and often bring me comfort as an adult.*

*There were times in my life that I let fear dissipate my energy.*

*The battles that I've gone through have often drained me, leaving me depressed and limp, vulnerable to the enemy.*

*It is in those times that I've experienced a manifestation of God like no other. When I can no longer think, I often conjure up those memories of my mother singing as she rocked in her chair.*

*One of the songs that I remember most, is a song called GOTT IST DIE LIEBE. This translates to GOD LOVES ME DEARLY. The song goes like this...*

*God loves me dearly,
Grants me salvation,
God loves me dearly,
Loves even me.*

*Refrain:
Therefore I'll say again:
God loves me dearly,
God loves me dearly,
Loves even me.*

*I was in slavery,
Sin, death, and darkness;
God's love was working
To make me free. [Refrain]*

*He sent forth Jesus,
My dear Redeemer;
He sent forth Jesus
And set me free. [Refrain]*

*Jesus, my Savior,
Himself did offer;
Jesus, my Savior,
Paid all I owed. [Refrain]*

*Now I will praise You,
O love Eternal;
Now I will praise You
All my life long. [Refrain]*

(Lyrics from a Luther Hymnal that was written in 1693 now public domain.)

Here I was, escorting my son to and from his court hearings. Although my heart was hurting, I found strength *in the words of this precious song passed down to me from my mother.*

*I was investing my energy in trusting Him and singing His Song. It was then that I could feel God working in my heart.*

*Exodus 15:2 KJV The LORD is my strength and song, and he is become my salvation: he is my God, and I will prepare him an habitation; my father's God, and I will exalt him.*

*Psalm 8:2 KJV Out of the mouth of babes and suckling's hast thou ordained strength because of thine enemies, that thou mightiest still the enemy and the avenger.*

*James 5:13 KJV is any one of you afflicted? Let him pray. Is anyone merry? Let him sing psalms.*

*The mind of sinful man is death, but the mind controlled by the Spirit is life and peace. Fill your heart and your spirit with the gift of song. There you will find your strength.*

*The book of Psalms is music and prophecy; music to rejoice by when your heart is glad, music to be comforted by when your heart is sad.*

*My dad (third from the left)*

## Day Nine
### *My Dad*

*My father was born in Russia. His first learned attitudes and beliefs were those of mistrust and uncertainty.*

*Carl was a stocky built man with black hair and brown eyes. He learned his trade of wood working from his grandfathers while they lived in Russia.*

*My dad grew up during a time of political unrest, not knowing when the Russian Army would break into their home at night, wake them up, and check their home for reasons unknown to this eight year old boy. But, because of this, Carl and his family learned to hide necessities in preparation for what could happen, and they became clever with their hiding places.*

*After arriving in America, My dad adjusted quickly in his new home and to the freedom of privacy and trust. He was confident in himself, loved to talk, was friendly to everyone, and opened his home to all without a formal invitation.*

*These new traits provided Carl the means to become successful as a farmer and in the construction business. He became known in the community for his unselfish generosity.*

*My father was not wealthy. However, he always shared his good fortune with others who were not as fortunate. As a child, I recall standing in line at the grocery store with my dad, when a woman in front of us began to cry. She did not have enough money to pay for the food she needed. Without a word, my father handed money to the clerk for this woman's groceries, and then he stepped back in line.*

*Although my father appeared to have adapted well in his new home, the life he had in Russia apparently left deep scars. He had learned early in life to prepare himself for an uncertain future. Upon Carl's death at age 75, his cache of food, clothes, and money was found hidden among his tools in the garage. My dad had still been waiting for the coming of the Russian Army.*

*My father left his children many wonderful memories, and he exemplified to both family and friends what it meant to be a Christian.*

## *Day Ten*
### *The Dreamer*

*Before we even get out of bed, he has already been working to prepare the path that will get us through the day. God has placed hidden treasures, strategically, throughout our day. Some of the treasures are trials that are designed to shake us free from our earthen-shackles.*

*My one and only son, also known as my favorite son, seemed to end up in the hospital every few months, running high fevers. The agony of a mother was watching the nurses bath my baby's body in ice water, and his little arms reaching out for me and crying for help. I couldn't rescue him. As a baby, he didn't understand why I couldn't help him.*

*It wasn't until we moved to Colorado Springs, and thanks to a competent doctor, we found out that Darin's white blood cell counts were low. My son formed a special bond with this doctor. This little boy, as soon as he learned how to use the phone, was able to call his doctor himself, and was always able to talk to him on the phone. This would be unheard of in today's world.*

*But it's nice to know that we can also call on our Heavenly Physician 24 hours a day. He is there to hear our concerns as easily as Darin learned to pick up the phone to call his favorite doctor.*

*Darin was always my dreamer, but we never knew what dreams were filtering out of his mind. He kept a lot in his head that he never shared. One day, I noticed he ran from our 8 track player, out in my garden, put his hand in the dirt, shook off the dirt, and ran back in to the 8 track player. After a few trips back and forth out to the garden, I question him as to what he was doing. He said," I want to grow up to be a big, big man." I finally attuned my ear, and listened to the words of that song, "You have to get a little dirt on your hand to grow up to be a big man." by Bill Anderson.*

*After that, he wanted his father to build him a rodeo fence. He would sit out on that fence, wearing a cowboy hat that his uncle Marvin had given him, and just gaze into his own little world.*

*My son, the dreamer, is now grown. He is the pastor of a church in Colorado. His dreams have also gotten bigger. He started a Biblically-based support group called "Heart*

*Revolution". It is a Christ centered organization that is designed to lead people to freedom from their addictions which include, drugs. alcohol, gangbangin, suicide, depression, etc.*

*God had to do a lot of work in Darin before this dream transpired. But, after the Lord got his attention, Darin made a promise that he would serve his Savior the rest of his days. My son has been obedient to the Lord, and his dreams are being fulfilled.*

*Were these parts of Darin's dreams while he sat on that fence as a kid, and did that dirt help make him the man he so desired to become?*

*Genesis 37 tells us that Joseph's dreams were that he would one-day rule over his brothers, and because of his brothers' jealousy, Joseph was sold into slavery. Later, Joseph was thrown into prison. Joseph went from being condemned in prison to being exalted to Pharaoh's right hand in a single day.*

*God has special plans for Darin, and it is God, alone, who has given Darin his dreams. God needed a man with hands that had a little dirt on them to do the work of the big man that God intended him to be.*

**(Photo taken by Chandra Bryan granddaughter of Joan)**

## *Day Eleven*
## *The Ultimate Weight Loss*
## *Forgiveness*

*We hear the word weight loss, and we immediately think of body weight.*

*I had been carrying around a weight on my shoulders for years. It was called "UNFORGIVENESS".
It is not easy to forgive, yet it is a burden, and it is a lot of weight to carry around.*

*Forgiveness is a way to unburden oneself from the constant pressure of rewriting the past. It's a gesture.*

*Let's face it. Each of us has been confronted by some pretty overwhelming challenges to forgive. Some seem...well, unforgivable. Sometimes the person who hurt us isn't sorry, or won't take responsibility, or is in the grave. The person*

*might be sorry, but refuses to recompense. Perhaps the person simply doesn't deserve our forgiveness. After all, forgiveness would make everything ok.
Forgiveness is for our own sakes, not the sake of the one who hurt us.*

*Jer. 31:34b
I will forgive their sins, and I will no longer remember their wrongs. I, the Lord, have spoken.*

*Perhaps the act of holding on to a rock may make the process of forgiveness very real. Holding on to hate, anger, and resentment is like clutching the rock. After a while, your hand hurts, and you can't do anything else. Forgiveness is like opening the hand, and in the case of us humans, opening the heart. The hurt stops, and you are free to do other things.*

*Even when we are taking our time in forgiving others, or ourselves, God's forgiveness is already there for us. All we have to do is accept God's forgiveness.*

*Forgiveness is not easy. It takes time, and it takes effort. Did you know that the ability to forgive others is a gift from God? The Bible tells us that if we don't forgive others, we cannot be forgiven. Unforgiveness blocks the ability for God to work in your life. When you choose to forgive, you are choosing God's way and opening the door for Him to heal your life.*

*Forgiveness does not mean what the other person did was right, or that you even have to get back into a relationship with that person. Forgiveness simply releases the debt they owe you, so that God can release the debt you owed Him. Ask the Lord to search your heart and show you if there is any unforgiveness blocking His blessing in your life. Ask*

*Him to show you more about this gift of forgiveness, so that you can walk in the freedom and blessing God has for you.*

*Unforgiveness is not attractive on anybody, and it does weigh you down. Get rid of all that weight of unforgiveness, and give it to the Lord.*

*Jer. 31:34b*
*I will forgive their sins and I will no longer remember their wrongs. I, the Lord, have spoken.*

## *Day Twelve*
## *The Road to Damascus*

*When I heard the message about God blinding Saul of Tarsus on the road to Damascus. I realized that God sometimes has to blind us to get our attention. For Paul it took 3 days. For some people, it can take months even years. I prayed that God would blind my son, Darin, to get his attention. Then I got angry with God.*

*You see, I didn't ask God to put my son in prison. I just wanted God to get his attention.*

*I realized years later that God had to back my son against a wall to get his attention, and unfortunately it took a prison wall to do it.*

*Not only did God get my son's attention like he did Paul's, but now my son has become an evangelist and pastor, like the apostle Paul.
The Lord doesn't just get our attention, and leave us wondering, he is specific with us.*

*Is God trying to get your attention? Listen!
Proverbs 3: 5, 6*

*Trust in the Lord with all your heart and lean not on your own understanding. In all thy ways acknowledge him, and he will make your paths straight.*

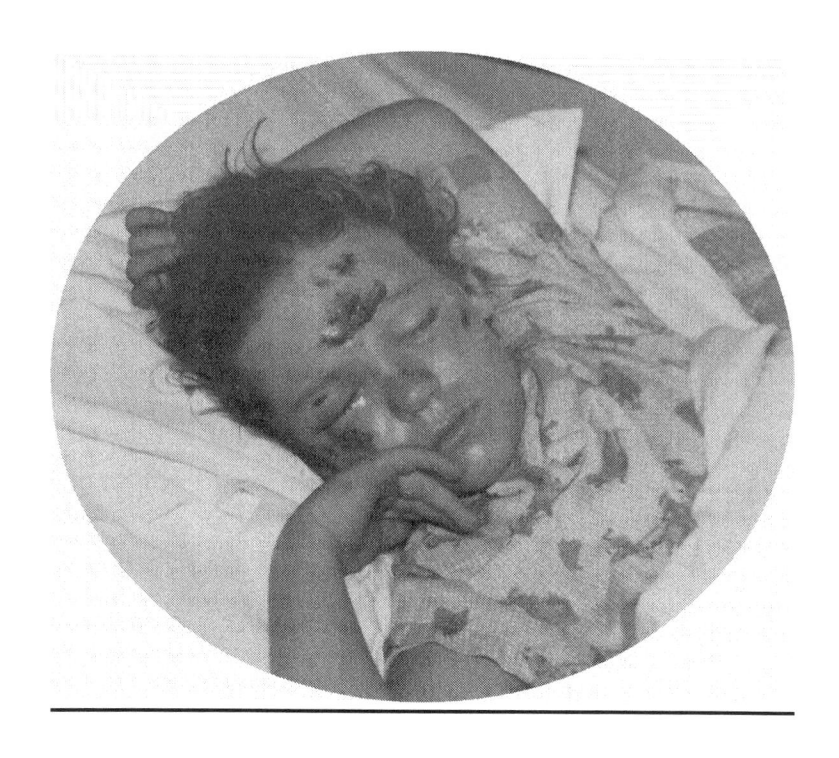

## *Day Thirteen*
## *Pacing the Hospital Floor Can be One of the Longest Days of Your Life.*

*Prayer was all I had to hang on to. When my baby, my youngest child, was hit by a homemade bomb. her face and body were embedded with shrapnel.*

*Why would someone place this bomb where there were children around?*

*The enemy attacked all three of my children. Why did God allow these things to happen to innocent children that belonged to him?*

*I remember Tona was so brave through it all. I had to remain strong for her. Only God could give me that strength.*

*Attacks from Satan, along with all other tribulations, can cause believers to draw closer to Christ, learn to resist Satan, practice patience, resist temptation, and grow stronger in our faith in many other ways.*

*God heard my prayers, and as each year passed, those scars on Tona's face and body, began to heal and became less and less visible.*

*One of my mother's favorite scriptures was Psalm 121, which we always said at home. This Scripture was what came to my mind while I was waiting the outcome of Tona's surgery.*

*Psalm 46:1 King James Version (KJV) God is our refuge and strength, a very present help in trouble.*

*5 For as the sufferings of Christ abound in us, so our consolation also abounds through Christ. 6 Now if we are afflicted, it is for your consolation and salvation, which is effective for enduring the same sufferings which we also suffer. Or if we are comforted, it is for your consolation and salvation. 7 And our hope for you is steadfast, because we know that as you are partakers of the sufferings, so also you will partake of the consolation.*

> Pride comes before the fall

## **Day Fourteen**
## *The Lesson*

*It is written, "pride will come before the fall," As understood and hated as this quality is by most people, many still succumb to its tempting and seductive nature, and many end up losing everything as a result of having a prideful holier than thou attitude.*

*This cancerous, and destructive quality, has brought down more kingdoms, caused more wars, destroyed more marriages, and has ruined more relationships than all of the other negative qualities combined.*

*I however, embraced this spirit of pride, and justified it as being a positive trait. I embraced it and thought of it perhaps as being one of my good qualities. You see, I grew up fearing God as well as my mother; therefore I stayed away from trouble.*

*I made the assumption that because I had taught my children right from wrong, and because I was a God fearing woman from a Christian home, that my children would grow up to be exceptional teens. I also found myself feeling perhaps a bit superior to my friends and family that were going through some difficult situations and circumstances. I felt I was exempt from all trouble simply because I was a good person.*
*God hates the spirit of pride.*

*Yes, pride, as in my case, comes before the fall.*

*Proverbs 16: 18 Pride goeth before destruction, and an haughty spirit before a fall.*

*Robert Koss my second husband*

## **Day Fifteen**
## Unconditional Love and Joy

God loves us SO much, and he LOVES and ACCEPTS us no matter what we've done, or what our past has been. He loves us, even if we can't love ourselves.

God shapes us and molds us into what he intended for our life.

My life was on a downward spiral, and things were getting worse, not better. Life was more than I could possibly bear, and I felt as if the hand of God left me. I wanted an easy way out, so I tried to take my own life. I attempted suicide. I wound up in a mental hospital, and for my own safety, was locked up.

Being locked up was a frightening and lonely experience. I was confused and heartbroken, and I really didn't want to go on living. I felt I had nothing to live for and no one to turn to for comfort.

It was in my darkest despair that I finally cried out to God, and in his small still voice, He reassured me that He had never left me, nor did He forsake me. That was such a comfort to me.

God will never leave us nor forsake us. Hebrews 13:5-6
This was how I felt when I met my husband. He was a well-respected man in our community, He saw me for whom I was, and he saw the person God intended me to be. I felt loved, and it was a good feeling. It brought me comfort and a sense of value.

Robert was a wonderful man and fun to be with. He taught me how to have fun, and enjoy life for what it was. He was always there encouraging me to be the best in everything I set out to do.

God places people in our lives for a reason. I know that God gave me this man for 11 years of my life, to help me with my walk in life, and to show me how to love once again.

I thank God for bringing me Robert. His memory still brings comfort and joy to me to this day.

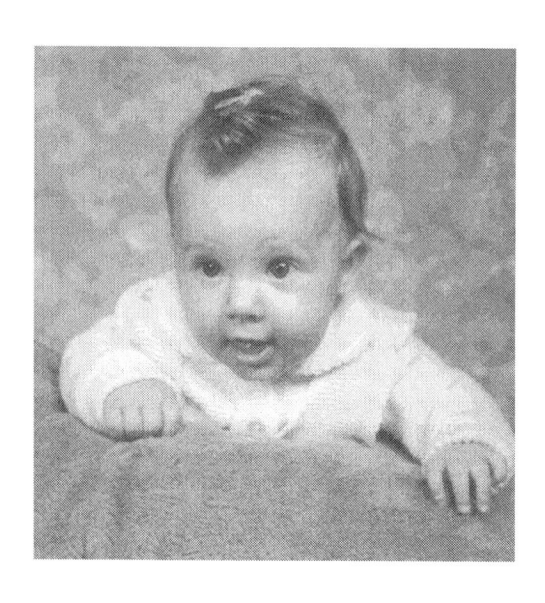

## *Day Sixteen*
### *My Youngest Daughter*

*When I held her and looked into her face, I knew that she was going to bring our family joy. She was a genuine gift from God, and I knew it.*

*Tona brings with her a sense of confidence and strength to all those who know her. Tona has been blessed with a calming spirit about her. She is one that her family and friends can always depend upon.*

*Although she has gone through life's trials herself, she always has a smile on her face, in spite of hard times. This child has brought our family strength through her positive attitude and sense of humor. I think God uses her as a reminder to me that life is so precious.*

*A person may encounter many obstacles as you move through life, but we must remember to never give up! God will hold our hand and walk with us, and at times he will even carry us. I need to be reminded to notice the times he carries me, and not be grumbling so loud that I don't even notice that he is CARRYING ME. He never leaves me to walk alone.*

## ***Day Seventeen***
*Seeking the Perfect World*

*Why do we always seem to feel that if we just had this or that, then the world would be perfect for us?*

*When our family had an opportunity to head for a bigger city, I was excited. My life was going to be filled with excitement; my dreams were going to be complete. I was young and seeking the perfect world.*

*The one thing needful that I didn't look for to complete my perfect world was GOD. Without God we have nothing. Even though I was brought up in a strict Christian home, somehow, I forgot about asking God to be part of my dream.*

*You see, we don't live in a perfect world...But, we do serve a perfect God.*

## *Day Eighteen*
## *Anticipation and Insecurity*

*2 days, 1 hour, 55 minutes, and counting; you know how you can get so excited over something that you find yourself actually counting down the hours and the minutes.*

*Your heart races because you are looking in anticipation towards that moment. That is how it felt when I found out my son would be released from prison.*

*God was the only one that knew how I felt on the inside. Only through God's grace, was his release accomplished.*

*But as his release date got closer, fear set in. I wondered, once released from prison, would my son continue to serve the Lord, or was this just some jail house religion he was going through?*

*"Who would hire a convict...much less, someone that had been in prison for manslaughter?"*

*I became confused. "Was the man that went in, the same person that came out?" This nervousness was bothersome to me.*

*""Is he going to fail? I needed to be there to encourage him no matter what, and reassure him that because of my love for him, that I would stand behind him.*

*Before my son went into prison, I prayed to God that he would change my son like he did Paul. I spent a lot of time reading Corinthians, and watching how God was answering my prayers.*

*My son did not know, until after he became a pastor, that I prayed for God to blind him like he did Paul. This is how God works. He takes everything that the devil tries to destroy and turns it around for his Glory.*

*In the midst of our insecurity, it can be difficult to "let go and let God". I still find myself struggling with this daily. Oh, it's easy to give it to God, but then I find myself spending the rest of the day, trying to figure out how I can make things happen. I continue to worry and fret over the outcome. The anticipation and worry of things to come are sometimes overwhelming.*

*But, rather than counting down the minutes, I've learned more peace comes to me if I simply begin counting my blessings.*

## *Day Nineteen*
## *My First Born*

*I remember when my daughter was born, my mother told me that this baby girl was a gift from God. Little did I realize what a gift she really was!*

*In the wee hours of the morning, I was awaken to the excitement of my precious two year old. She stood beside my bed telling me that Jesus had come to see her.*

*Now, normally this child was incredibly frightened of the dark, and would never have ventured down the hallway to my room without crying out for me to turn on the lights. Stunned, I asked her if He talked to her. She said, "No, He was just standing there beside my bed."*

*As a mother, I felt comforted by the fact that I knew that she was in the hands of Jesus. I also wondered, in the back of*

*my mind, "Did this mean that I might lose my little girl? Was this some sign that He was going to be taking her?" Fourteen years later, once again in the wee hours of the morning, I awoke only to discover that she had been kidnapped. Those feelings of both fear and of comfort crept back. I had the comfort of knowing that Jesus was there holding her hand, but was I was frightened. Did this mean that she might never come back home? I knew in my heart, that was a possibility, and I knew that I had to trust God. After all, my daughter belonged to Christ, and I trusted Him and knew I'd have to accept either fate.
Loss can come upon you suddenly and overwhelm you with grief.*

*She carried the trauma of that kidnapping experience with her for years. But what the devil tries to destroy, God will take and use for his Glory.*

*Later in her years, she and her husband became foster parents. My darling daughter wanted to save every child from the evils of the world. She made sure that each one of her children was raised in Sunday School and with the knowledge of God's word because she wanted them to know the Jesus that has been so real in her life. She has spent a life time caring for children, volunteering, reaching out, and telling others about Jesus.*

*Lamentations 3 gives us hope for the grieving.
"In your darkest times, do your thoughts turn to God?"*

Pikes Peak, as seen from Garden of the Gods photographed by Beverly Lussier

## *Day Twenty*
*"Be Still and Know that I Am God"*
*Psalm 46: 10*

*Be still and let God. God's love and healing power rush in when I become still. I'm learning to rest in the stillness of God.*

*Have you ever gazed across the sky and marveled at the things of God?*

*Have you ever listened to God as you watched the waves of the ocean in amazement?*

*Have you ever felt the warmth of the sun caressing your skin on a hot summer day?*

*I remember enjoying the drive to work, in the early morning hours when I lived back in Colorado Springs. Seeing the majestic purple mountains was breath taking. If those mountains could speak, they would tell tales of miracles, victories, and defeats, and whisper the quiet reverence of God's presence.*

*The beautiful snowcapped mountains are a peaceful picturesque sight, handcrafted by God, Himself. I can still envision that majestic scene in my mind, and it will always remind me of the power, creativity, and serenity of the almighty God.*

*Ask the Holy Spirit to sharpen your spiritual mind, so that you can see the beauty and handiwork that God surrounds us with each day. Practice looking and listening during these quiet times.*

*Psalm 8: 1-4
The Heavens declare the glory of God.*

## Day Twenty-One
## Brazil

*Luke 11:28 reminds us that we need to obey the word of God.*

*Listening to God's word was something I once took for granted and often ignored.*

*When a pastor gave me a word that I would be teaching women and reaching people all over the world, I chose to ignore his prophecy. I assumed that the message was not truly meant for me. After all, I wasn't qualified, or so I felt.*

*Four years later, while in Brazil on a mission trip, a visiting pastor from Singapore approached me with the same message as the pastor from United States had given me.*

*Twice God had given me that message, once in my own country, and the second from another country. It didn't matter where I was, God knew where I was, and he was trying to get my attention.*

*He wanted me to be obedient to His word, but instead, I let fear and doubt set in. I guess I was acting a bit like Jonah did when he was asked to go to Ninevah.*

*My original thoughts were that I didn't have the qualification to be teaching anyone, so I chose to ignore these messages.*

*Then He spoke to me, and reminded me of the pain, fears, and doubts I had experienced in my life. Those experiences are what qualified me for what God wanted me to do, but He needed for me to trust in Him and to be obedient. The plan God had for me began to unfold. I began to understand that He wanted me to listen and comfort others in ways a Bible teacher or professional theologian never could unless they'd been there.*

*God did help me through all of my crisis and pain. I discovered that my testimony and my experiences are an example of the faithfulness of God.*

*The only qualification that God required was my willingness. I needed only to be a willing vessel. God does the rest.*

*Throughout the Bible, God chose leaders that weren't qualified, but He chose people whose heart he could work with. All he wants from us is to be obedient.*

*Paul tells us in his writing to the Colossians that the message doesn't diminish or weaken over time. It's the same all over the world.*

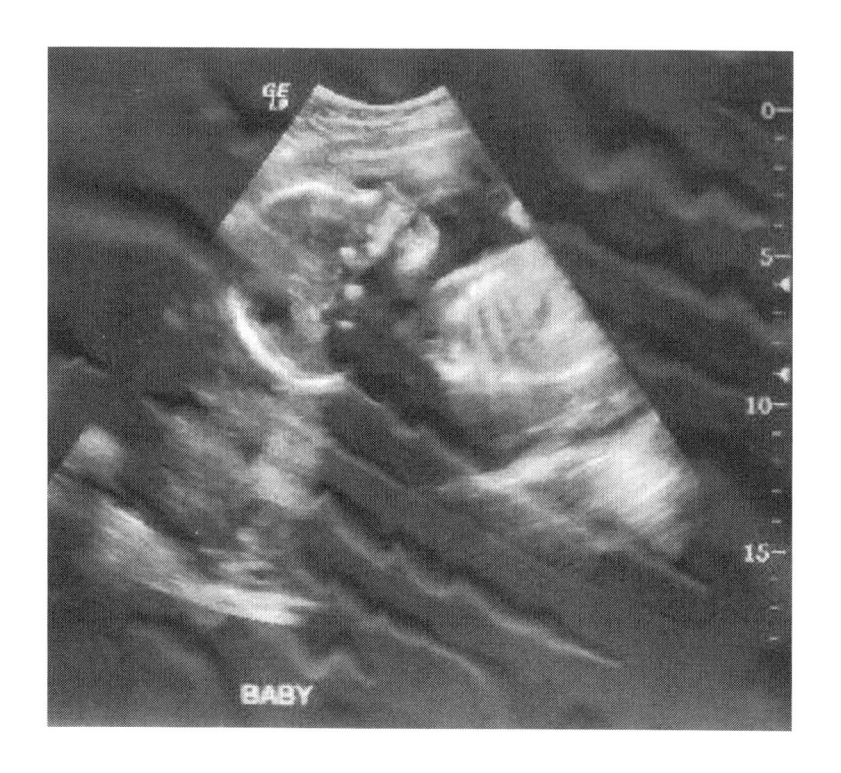

## *Day Twenty-Two*
## *The Heart Beat that Changes Everything*

*My family was complete with what I felt was a perfect family, a daughter and a son. Wow, I couldn't ask for anything more.*

*That's why I was stunned when I learned that I was pregnant for a third time. All I could do was cry. In fact, I think the doctor got so tired of me crying in his office, that he asked if I wanted an abortion. I think hearing that brought me out of the selfishness that I was feeling.*

*I couldn't do that. There was a life growing inside of me, so I decided to move forward with the pregnancy.*

*With my other two pregnancies, my child birth had been a breeze, but I had difficulty with Tona's birth. When she was born, the doctor and nurses called it a LOP (Left Occiput Posterior) birth.*

*This unexpected gift became our joy. The moment we brought our baby home, she knew she was loved and wanted. My oldest daughter was thrilled and even asked to keep the crib in her room. She loved having a baby sister. Between her and my son, this baby found out she had the rule of the roost.*

*She grew up with confidence, and has always shown strength and character. Even when she was facing surgery during her bomb explosion, it was evident that God had graced her with strength from above.*

## *Day Twenty-Three*
### *Sitcom*

*I remember when I was a kid growing up, I used to try to visualize what my future would be like.*

*Like most people I got my reference and ideas from watching **TV sitcoms such as:** Ozzie and Harriet, Father Knows Best, The Andy Griffin Show, and Leave it to Beaver.*

- *These TV shows were my first role models of an American family.*
- *They presented life at its best.*
- *In every 30 minute segment, all of life's problems could be handled and resolved around the kitchen table.*

*Funny, but a part of me thought this was real life.*

*Part of me still wishes it were. But the reality is, sometimes life hands you situations that cannot be solved in a matter of minutes.*

*I grew up in the late 50's in a little country town, and I yearned for the big city life,*

*After I'd married my husband, we had an opportunity to head for a bigger city. We jumped at the chance. Oh, was I excited! My life was going to be filled with new adventures!*

*My dreams were going to be complete. I was thrilled. I was young, and I had high hopes and great dreams. I was seeking the perfect world.*

*Well, my life started out with what I felt was perfection.*

*God blessed me with three beautiful children. I felt on top of the world when my oldest daughter, Teila won the title of "Colorado Ideal Miss Teenager". But that excitement soon led to horror, when she was held at gun point, kidnapped, assaulted, and shot.*

*Wait! This couldn't be happening. I was a good person. I was a Christian, and no, this was not what I had planned for my life.*

*I didn't remember anything like this nightmare I was experiencing, happening in any of those sitcoms. On TV, everything was resolved around a kitchen table usually in 30 minutes or less.*

*Instead of sitting around a table, I found myself sitting in a courtroom listening to the pain that my daughter had to endure.*

*My daughter's experiencing all of this horror wasn't part of my dream.*

*In difficult times, it can be hard to trust God. All I could do was pray to God for comfort. Inside, I felt I had failed as a mother, and I began to blame myself.*

*My husband, on the other hand, began drinking alcohol to hide his pain.*

*I hadn't even recovered from my daughter's kidnapping when I found myself pacing the hospital floor, and praying for a miracle. I was in the hospital, waiting for my youngest daughter, Tona, to get out of surgery. She had been hit by a homemade bomb, and her face was shattered. She had shrapnel splattering hitting her and tearing into her fragile body. By that time, I realized that life's problems could not be resolved around that kitchen table. This was not a reality that I had prepared myself for. I was not living a TV sitcom life, and my trials and tribulations were not going to be resolved in a 30 minute episode. When this happen to my baby, my husband felt that he had an excuse to drink even more, and once again, I knew I failed as a mother and as a wife.*

*I just knew June Cleaver or Harriet Nelson would have known exactly what to do, but I didn't.*

*The communication between my husband and me continued to break down as we went through the ordeal of nearly losing our girls.*

*His drinking grew worse and the beatings started. After I survived a collapsed lung from one of his beatings, he informed me that he wanted a divorce.*

*My perfect life, that I had imagined, didn't exist. Just when I didn't think things could get any worse, THEY DID. I didn't have the advantage of a remote control to fast forward to get beyond all of this.*

*Aunt Bea, from the Andy Griffin Show, never stopped by with a cup of tea, to help me solve my problems or to dry my tears. I was ALONE, or so I thought*

*I didn't feel I had anyone that I could turn to. I thought if this is how the rest of my life would be, one tragedy after another, I didn't want to be here.*

*My spirit was broken, and I wanted an easy way out, so I tried to kill myself.*

*Because of that suicide attempt, they locked me up in a mental ward. My husband had me committed.*

*When someone else commits you, it is not that easy to get out.*

*When I heard the door lock behind me, I felt I had been betrayed and abandoned.*

*I felt so helpless, not to mention how terrified, I felt being isolated in such a scary place.*

*When my kids came to visit me in the hospital, they told me, "Mom if you would have died, we would have stomped on your grave." (They were so hurt.)*
*Now, I felt that even my kids had rejected me. At this point, I really felt alone. I didn't even feel that God was there for me.*

*After days of crying and questioning God, and asking, "God, where are you? Don't you see that I'm hurting? Do you even care that I hurt?"*

*I expressed my pain, my hurt, the rejections from everyone, and vented my sorrow of feeling abandoned by everyone. Yes, I felt abandoned by everyone, including God. This was probably the most honest I that I had ever been with God.*

*With every word and with every tear, I could feel the spirit of God pouring over me.*

*I heard a small, still voice saying, "Joanie, I didn't leave you. I'm right here with you."*

*God was watching over me, and He was in control in my life.*

*I knew then that my almighty God would be the only one who could get me out of this place. He was already working behind the scenes.*

*I was locked up, but Jesus had the key to let me out, not man.*

*A head nurse on the floor realized that my husband was trying to undermine me, so she had my psychiatrist replaced with a Christian counselor. It was because of him that I was finally released.*

*Isn't it funny how we can blame God when things go wrong? We give up on even offering prayer to God. But when the road gets tougher, we know that God is the only one we know we can turn to. God is so good, because He is always is there for us, just waiting for us to call out to him. In a split second, He is there comforting us.*

*I learned years later that my children were there for me every step of the way, but because of my emotional state, I did not remember any of this.*

*I had been unable to see or feel their frustration in trying to help me. I only turned my back on their help.*

*I had no idea how my actions hurt my children. The rejection they felt when I tried to take my own life, left them feeling abandoned, disillusioned, and having to carry this burden of guilt that I put upon them.*

*I'll never know the full damage that I placed on my children through my selfish actions.*

*Through a long process, and many hours of prayer, God restored my hope and painted in my life a brighter future. God also blessed me with a new husband.*

### **HOWEVER, SATAN WASN'T FINISHED WITH MY FAMILY.**

*My son, Darin, had stopped attending church. He was now taking drugs, dealing drugs, and had joined a gang.*

*During a party, where drugs and alcohol were being used, a gun went off, killing a young girl, and Darin was arrested for murder.*

*With my son's name and photo in every shocking headline splattered across all newspapers, and every TV and radio station airing the news, every day for days, I isolated myself from everyone at work.*

*I hid from the neighbors. I avoided people at the stores*

*The shame was too much. I couldn't face my friends or family.*

## ***Our family FINALLY MADE IT ON TV, BUT IT WASN'T IN A SITCOM.***

*Before the shooting incident occurred, one day while driving to work, I turned on the radio and heard a pastor speaking on how God had to blind Paul on that road to Damascus to get his attention. He went on to say, that God blinds us sometime for hours, days, weeks, and even years to get our attention.*

*I immediately prayed that God would blind my son, Darin, like he did Paul on that road to Damascus, and that he would lead Darin back to God, himself. I had no idea that God was already way ahead of me and was going to answer my prayers in a most unimaginable way.*

*I didn't mean that I wanted you to send my son to prison, Lord. That isn't what I meant when I prayed that prayer.*

*I realized later that God needed to back my son up against a wall to get his attention. Unfortunately it took a prison wall.*

*God not only got Darin's attention, but if you remember after Paul recovered, he went on to be the first evangelist. Likewise, my son, Darin, just like Paul, became a pastor, and an evangelist.*

*He is proof that God can and does change people.*

*When Darin was released from prison, he was reunited with his wife, Gloria, and his daughter Chandra. However, things weren't back to normal.*

*Their kitchen table still held painful, unspoken memories that did not resolve themselves overnight much less in 30 minutes, as they should have if life were a sitcom. When Darin went to prison, he left his family with a lot of open wounds and heartaches.*

*Even though his daughter missed him and loved to visit him in prison, she was not quite ready to receive him back home once he'd been released.*

*When Darin was released from prison, Chandra stood in the doorway. She put her hands up, and told her mom that she was stupid, for allowing her dad to come back into their home.*

*The pain and hurt was still too fresh in her mind. She cried herself to sleep many nights.*

*The pain did not go away overnight for anyone. The pain Darin felt being rejected by his daughter, stabbed him deep, but he knew he had to bear the pain, and try to build back that trust.*

*It was not easy for Darin to readjust to life outside of prison community. People from the church were not eager to accept him either.*

*But, because of the faithfulness of God, Darin's family situation has been restored and healed.*

*Darin made a promise to always serve God in his life and with God's help, he has kept that promise.*

*After a few years, once again, my faith was shaken. My wonderful new husband, of 11 years, whom God so richly blessed me with, had a heart attack and died, leaving me a widow. God in his infinite wisdom, knew I could serve Him in a greater sense, and have a much richer life, even with my new situation as a widow.*

*Looking back, I think I sometimes still wish that all of life's problems could be resolved in a matter of 30 minutes around that kitchen table that seemed to have some magical healing powers.*

*But the best place I found to resolve my issues were on my knees in prayer and in the word of God. My God was the only one I could really trust to heal every situation and stand by my side.*

*My ideal family was based on a sitcom that didn't exist, but my God is real.*

*My kitchen table was not always a place of refuge, much less a peace keeping table. Our home was, at times, our own battleground.*

*God is faithful, and he brought me through all of the toughest trials in my life. When I surrendered my will and ask God for direction and peace, He worked a miracle in my home and in my heart.*

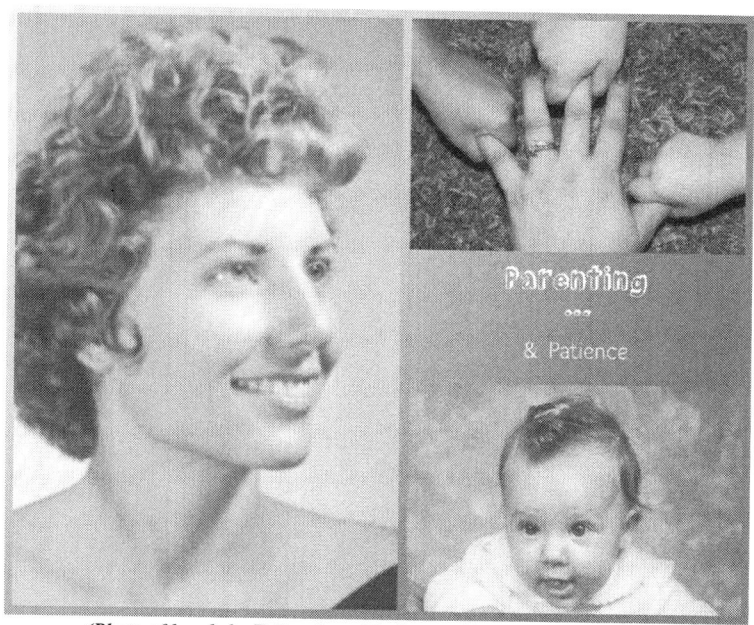

*(Photo of hands by Tylina Joan Havle granddaughter of Joan Koss)*

# *Day Twenty-Four*
## *Parenting and Patience*

*Jesus took time out of His busy schedule to stop and bless the children. Jesus was a good example of how we should always be to our children.*

*Children are a heritage, a reward from God.
I had a long hard day at work, and came home to start my daily routine of fixing dinner for my family. There I found my youngest child in the middle of the floor with the TV blasting and all of her stuff strung out on the floor.
She looked up at me with her dynamic smile as to let me know she was glad to see me. She has always radiated a confident, peaceful, personality.*

*Yet, even with that precious smile, I lost it. My house was a mess, and I was upset. I began to take out my frustration on her, yelling at her for the mess she had made.*

*That smile she was wearing just moments earlier disappeared, and she burst into tears, saying, "Fine, I had a rough day at school, now my own mom is giving me a rough time at home." Those words pierced my soul, and I knew I had to ask God to forgive me for not approaching my daughter with a hug and letting her know I was glad to see her.*

*Mothers have an awesome responsibility. God gives us children, and we are to protect them, nourish them, and love them. But sometimes we let the devil control us. I encourage all mothers to not take your children for granted. Remember, they are a precious gift from God, and we need to treat them with respect.*

*I've learned that when I am tired or stressed, it's never acceptable to take that frustration out on children. The Bible reminds us in Colossians 3:21 to not provoke your children and crush their spirits.*

*Mothers, don't live with that guilt as I have. I have learned that you must ALWAYS talk to God and ask for guidance. Yes, we have the time. He is right there with us. We do not have to stop what we are doing and get on our knees. We can just talk to him while we are cooking or cleaning. After all, He is right there beside us, so carry on conservation with Him. In fact, He may show you a thing or two about household chores. I have learned to even ask God where I have misplaced something. The neat thing is, He immediately shows me in my head where it is. Remember to always give Him the credit for that, and thank Him. Learn to talk to Him as if you're talking to your husband, children, or a friend.*

*God will help you raise your children. Never stop asking Him for advice. Seek His word, and find out how to take care of what He has given us.*

*Provoking your children can destroy them, so place your children's hand, into God's hands.*

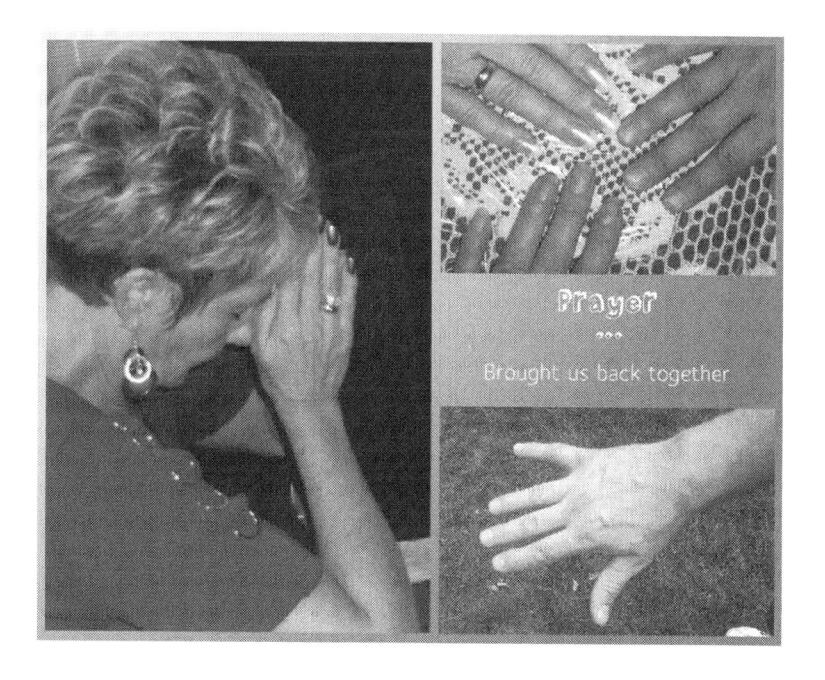

Prayer
...
Brought us back together

## *Day Twenty-Five*
*Living Water*

*When Bob and I left Colorado to move to Arizona, I imagined that this was going to be a fresh and new start. I could leave my past behind. No one in Arizona would know what I had gone through in life.*

*At that time, I had a lot of unforgiveness that I had not dealt with. I hadn't really forgiven Teila's kidnapper, nor the guy who placed the bomb that hurt Tona, and I hadn't forgiven my son, Darin, for the shame he brought to the family. I was also bitter and angry towards his drug addicted habit that had over shadowed his life and altered his thinking.*

*Most of all, I hadn't forgiven myself for all the hurt and shame that I brought to my kids when I attempted suicide. My selfishness blinded me.*

*I was reminded about the woman at the well. Jesus knew everything about her. God knows each of us individually. He knows our name and even how many hairs are on our head.*

*Who was I kidding, thinking that moving out of state would change circumstances and that God would not have me deal with my unforgivness.*

*Jesus offered the woman at the well "The Living Water", but somehow the woman missed the point of what Jesus was saying to her.*

*Jesus told her, "Go call your husband and come back". He touches the most sensitive and vulnerable spot in her life. The quickest way to the heart is through a wound.*
*To move forward, she needed to confront her past and her present. She saw that Jesus knew the truth about her, that the man she was with was not her husband.*

*John chapter 4, also tells us that the woman left her water jar behind, went into town, and told everyone about the Messiah.*

*What did it mean when she left her water jar behind? For me, it meant that when I left Colorado, I could not leave all my past there without dealing with my unforgiveness and guilt.*

*My water jug was filled with anger, rejection, hurt, unforgiveness. The list goes on and on. My water jug was not filled with "Living Water." This weight that we have in our water jug gets pretty heavy, and it slows us down. Yet, we long for a time of happiness and a fulfillment of life. We have such an important message to share with others. Jesus wants us to lay aside every weight that would hinder us from getting closer to Him.*

*Let the water jug represent that area of your life you want to leave behind and forget. In your mind's eye, take that water jar, and all it represents to you, and leave it behind with Jesus.*

*When we get filled with "Living Water," we will notice that God's voice gets clearer, as we clean our minds of worry, of anxious thoughts, or whatever else we have entangled in our brains. We now can let God's word reprogram our brains. Deuteronomy 30:20 tells us to "listen to His voice."*

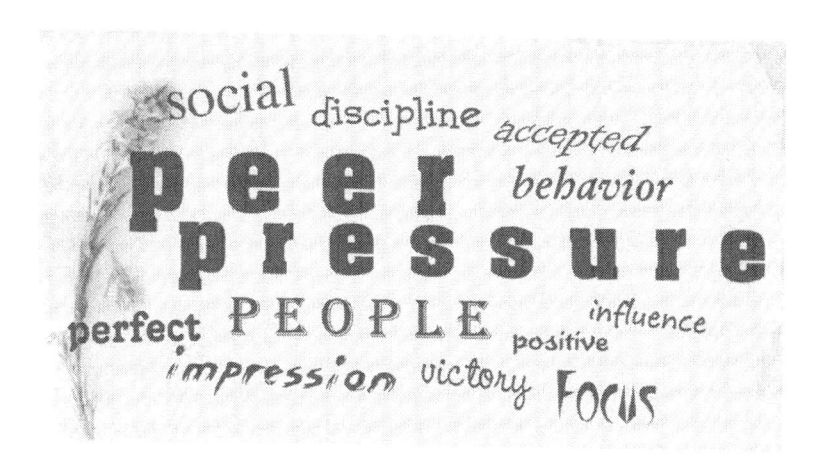

## Day Twenty-Six
### Peer Pressure

*Sometimes in life, we let other people influence us. Often, that hinders us from being what God wants us to be.*

*King David was not truly qualified to be a king over Israel, in man's eyes. Even his own father didn't think that he was a candidate to be King. In fact, his father sent all of his sons except David, to go before Samuel to be interviewed for this elite position.*

*But David had a heart that God could work with. His outward appearance did not make an overpowering first impression, but that wasn't what God was looking for. God uses a different standard of measurement than man uses. I Samuel 17:40 tells us that David picked up five smooth stones to fight Goliath. He only needed one, but choosing five was symbolic of David's preparation for victory. When David ran toward Goliath, he didn't see Goliath. His focus was on God.*

*The battle was not David's, and he knew it. Start letting the Lord step into your battle, and you will see victory.*
*I believe that while I was raising my kids, my focus was in wanting my kids to be perfect, to be smarter than others, and to be something they didn't want to be. I should have been more concerned with preparing their hearts to be what God wanted them to be.*

*I was more concerned with man's standards. God's opinion is the only one that matters.*

*We all face those monumental problems or run into impossible situations at one time or another. When we do, we must remember to STOP and refocus. God will fight our battles.*

*God never intended for us to have to face our trials alone. He is there at all times, waiting for us to call upon Him for the guidance, encouragement, and direction we need.*

## **Day Twenty-Seven**
*My Family*

*There is nothing like the peacefulness of a sleeping baby. When my children were babies, I would put them down for a nap. When I would go to check in on them later, nine times out of ten, I couldn't help myself. I just had to pick them up, cradle them in my arms, and hold them close to my heart.*

*Now that they are older, married, and have children of their own, I still look back to the time when they were babies. Did my love change over time, or did it change because of things they did that were wrong? NO. In fact, my love for them became even deeper over time. I have come to know them, not just as my children, but as children of the most high God. I gave birth to them, but God molded their lives, gave them each a unique quality, and equipped them with talents that they are now using that make them who they are.*

*Teila is an author, and has written several books. She graciously worked alongside me to help me write this one. She was a foster parent, and has helped rescue many children from the evils of the world. I sit back and marvel at how this woman could do that. Despite the trials that she had to endure, God found a way to use them for his Glory. He knew that someday, she would be out there to help other children. Had she not been kidnapped, she may not have had the desire to try and rescue other children.*

*Darin has become a minister. The love and the compassion he has for all who enter his church is phenomenal. Had he not made a commitment to serve the Lord while in prison, he may not have had the desire to tell others what the Lord can do to change their lives. He has written a book, "Torn Apart/Restored", about his life.*

*Tona is working for a corporation doing research for lawyers to help ensure that their case law citations are still current. The scars on her face are barely visible, but she is truly an example to others. Although her face was shattered and scarred, it made no difference. It was not the scars that defined her, it was God that designed her, and made her who she is.*

*Tona has a genuine joy from within, and her smile beams from the inside out. With time, God healed her scars, as he is the healer of all things.*

*If you ask me which one of my kids I am the most proud of, I would have to say "ALL THREE OF THEM". The three of them shine in my heart and in my eyes.*

*Oh, yes, there were times that I got angry and found myself disappointed with them, but never could I have turned my back on them. They were given to me as a gift from God.*

*John 6:37 tells us that whosoever comes to Him, He will never drive away.*

*Jesus also tells us in Matthew 19:14, "Let the little children come to him, because the kingdom of heaven belong to them." When my children call me, they playfully say to me, "Hi, Mom, it's your favorite child calling." I remind my son, that he is my favorite son. My daughter, Tona, is my favorite baby girl, and Teila, is my favorite oldest daughter.*

*Even though my children all grown, that doesn't keep me from trying to be their mother. But I have learned that it's God whom they really need.*

*(Lil top row third from the left and Joan is sitting on her mother's lap)*

## ***Day Twenty-Eight***
*My Sister, Lil*

*Growing up with a large family can have its challenges, but toss in five brothers, and life becomes even more challenging.*

*My sister, Lil, was double dared by her brothers to dive from the roof of what we called our well house. Even though it wasn't a tall building, (more like the height of a shed) they dared her to climb to the top and jump in the shallow horse trough below.*

*My sister, Lil, took them up on the challenge and proceeded to take off her clothes. She knew she'd be in trouble if her clothes were wet. She climbed to the top of the well house to show her brothers that she was tough.*

*Our mother just happened to see her as she was getting ready to jump, and her heart nearly leaped out of her body, visualizing what would happen to Lil if she performed this little foolish act.*

*Mom was not too happy with her little stunt. Although my brothers were the ones who had provoked her, in our mother's eyes, her boys, our brothers, could do no wrong. Therefore, Lil was going to get the spanking.*

*Since Lil was the princess in our father's eyes, Dad came to her rescue. He thought the boys should be the ones to get the punishment. I don't remember who won, our mom or our dad, but as I look at Lil's life, 70 some years later, now living with Alzheimer's, I know that it's her Heavenly Father who is watching out for her.*

*Our parents brought us up in a strict Christian, loving home, and gave us our base foundation to serve and honor God. Lil has lived her entire life for the Lord, going to church, attending Bible studies, and praying.*

*Does her faith in God remain alive even though her brain is slowing dying? I would like to think so. Just as her earthly father was there to save her from punishment, I know her Heavenly Father is there to rescue her from the gates of hell, and escort her into Heaven's pearly gates with Him. The disease does not kill the soul.*

*Roman 8:38, 39 tells us*
*For I am persuaded, that neither death, nor life, nor angels, nor principalities, nor powers, nor things present, nor things to come, (39) nor height, nor depth nor any other creature, shall be able to separate us from the love of God, which is in Christ Jesus our Lord.*

## *Chapter Twenty-Nine*
## *Golf*

*Golf is stupid! How can anyone become so preoccupied with chasing a little white ball around a field? This was my attitude for many years until my husband, Bob, approached me with the idea of taking golf lessons.*

*I gave the idea a LOT of thought, and surprisingly enough, I became intrigued. Playing golf made sense when I considered the environment, atmosphere, and the fun that I was having.*

*God's command is, "Set your mind on these things." Our thought pattern is so ingrained in us that it is sometimes impossible for us to change. Satan knows how to get us to "set our minds" his way. To me, I didn't even like watching golf on TV, much less want to learn how to play it. I had negative preconceived notions in my head that golf was stupid.*

*If I hadn't given golf a chance, I would have miss out on spending valuable time with my husband, the short time that I had him on this earth, and I would have missed the beauty of God's Earth. God's beauty is omnipresent.*

*I can see and appreciate God's handiwork on the golf course, from the cool breezes, the beautiful green grasses, to the people I meet on the golf course. When I'm out on the course, I always find myself thanking God for this wonderful sport that allows me the time to relax and to be among friends.*

*Playing in Kona, Hawaii by the ocean, is one of the most beautiful and relaxing places to be. God seems to speak to me through the gentle roar of the rushing waves of that mighty Pacific Ocean.*

*If I hadn't changed my attitude on golf, I wouldn't have had the opportunity to meet my friend, Marilyn, or to be able to have had the opportunities to play on her beautiful golf course by the Pacific Ocean.*

*I have met many Christians on different golf courses. Marilyn was even so kind as to share her family with me. Her sister, JoAnn, is a wonderful Christian, who has become part of my family as well. God does not place one person in our life that he hasn't put there for a reason. Looking back, I wonder how many more opportunities I missed out on that God had in store for me. My stubborn attitude of not wanting to reach out and learn something new has kept me from discovering exciting experiences. We face choices everyday regarding our attitude. How are we going to embrace them?*

*The most important thing is to give God the credit for all things, including golf. By the way, that little ball I chase around on the golf course comes in other colors besides white.*

## *Day Thirty*
### *What's in a Name?*

*I always wanted grandchildren, but I don't know what I looked forward to more, holding these little ones for the first time, or hearing them call me "Grandma", a name and title that I cherished.*

*As we grandmas know, when our precious ones come into this world, they develop their own vocabulary, and eventually tag you with their own unique name that they create just for "you."*

*When my two oldest grandchildren, Tylina and Chandra, were born, I was elated.*

*Tylina was Teila's first born, and Chandra was Darin's firstborn. I couldn't wait for them to call me Grandma.*

*Did these two call me Grandma? NO! Their name for me was "Mamu". It soon grew on me. When these precious girls reached out their arms and called me "Mamu", my heart melted.*

*Teila's second son, Jeremiah, was the first of my grandchildren to officially acknowledge me as Grandma. Finally I had become "Grandma", and I just loved hearing that name.*

*That title, "Grandma," carried on, and the name seemed to stick. I was "Grandma" to Teila's daughters, Tanisha and Darleen, and to her son, Robert. However, when they adopted Mark, he embraced me with yet another title. I became known to him as, "Grandma, my bestest friend". This was quite a mouth full for this little guy, who was developmentally delayed. It was a name that he created for me all on his own.*

*This was very interesting to me how these little babies can develop their own names for those that they love. Tona's daughter, Desirea, calls me "Grandma Joan", but Gloria and Darin's son, Lil D, who is 17 years younger than his sister Chandra, calls me "Grandma".*

*Did it make any difference that my first two granddaughters didn't call me "Grandma"? NO! Their name for me was unique, and I began to feel honored. In their own way, they had not only given me a special name, but the name they chose for me also brought joy to me.*

*Interestingly, my first great grandson, Talon, began calling me "Shishi", and that is exactly what his siblings, Dylan, Rylie, Baily, Billy, and Natalie began calling me as well. To this day, I have no idea how Talon came up with that, but it stuck.*

*Tanisha's first born, my great granddaughter, Tiarra, broke with tradition and adapted her own spin on things, calling me "Get out of town Grandma".*

*When she was just a year or two of age, I had difficulty understanding her gibberish, so in response to everything she'd say, I'd laughingly say, "Get Out of Town". I never thought that saying those words would eventually be tagged onto my name. But, that is how she remembered me, and it has become another title that I've been branded with, but do so cherish.*

*Tiarra's younger sister, Tristyn, is not talking yet, so I'm waiting to see what name she attaches to me.*

*My grandson, Jeremiah and his wife Shannon have two beautiful little girls, Khloé and Miah. Hopefully, when he returns home from Iraq, I will be able to meet Miah and Khloé. These two little cuties have no clue that I will be anxiously awaiting to hear the name they have chosen for me.*

*Darin's daughter, Chandra, now has a son, named Shelton, who isn't old enough yet to give me a title either, but I'm grateful that God has blessed me with grandchildren and great grandchildren.*

*It doesn't matter anymore that they don't ALL call me "Grandma". I have actually embraced all my names. As much as I love to hear the word "Grandma", I also love to hear my special names, as I know these names all have a special meaning to me.*

*In the old Testament God was given several different names as well. These names identify God and describe his character. He loves it when we call upon His name and use His names in our worship! I hope that you, too, will find these names a benefit to your spiritual life.*

*A Few Hebrew Names and Their Meanings*
*Adonai-Jehovah -- The Lord our Sovereign*
*El-Elyon -- The Lord Most High*
*El-Olam -- The Everlasting God*
*El-Shaddai -- The God Who is Sufficient*
*for the Needs of His People*
*Jehovah-Elohim -- The Eternal Creator*
*Jehovah-Jireh -- The Lord our Provider*
*Jehovah-Nissi -- The Lord our Banner*
*Jehovah-Ropheka -- The Lord our Healer*
*Jehovah-Shalom -- The Lord our Peace*
*Jehovah-Tsidkenu -- The Lord our Righteousness*
*Jehovah-Mekaddishkem -- The Lord our Sanctifier*
*Jehovah-Sabaoth -- The Lord of Hosts*
*Jehovah-Shammah -- The Lord is Present*
*Jehovah-Rohi -- The Lord our Shepherd*
*Jehovah-Hoseenu -- The Lord our Maker*
*Jehovah-Eloheenu -- The Lord our God*

*Spending time with God & Family .... Grandpa Bob*

Fishers of Men
Matthew
4:18-23

## ***Day Thirty-One***
*Gone Fishing*

*Years ago, I heard a song called, "God Loves to Talk to Little Boys While They're Fishin" by William J. and Gloria Gaither. Listening to the words of that song, gave me an appreciation as to why my husband, Bob, must have loved fishing.*

*When Bob's three children, Tami, Rob, and Daryl, were growing up, Bob loved to take them fishing. He could hardly wait to take his grandson, Matthew, on his first fishing trip. It brought Bob great joy when Matthew was finally old enough to head for the clear mountain streams with his grandpa.*

*It was an opportunity for Bob to spend some quality, one-*

*on-one time with his first grandson. The two went on to form a special bond through those fishing trips. I'd like to think that Bob passed on his appreciation for nature to Matthew. The Colorado mountains are a perfect place to spend time with a grandson and with the Lord.*

*Perhaps Bob wanted Matt to see these God made mountains for a reason, and to experience the tranquility of the crystal clear Colorado streams. It was a chance for the two of them to tap into the presence of God as they cast their lines into the waters.*

*(Psalm 127) Children are God's; we "inherit" them from him, to bring up and hold in trust. They are gifts, rewards; our lives are filled by being poured out for them."*

*Bob loved his grandchildren. I don't remember if Bob took his granddaughter, Dana, fishing or not, but I know that this cute little blond girl had a contagious smile that brought such joy to her grandpa. In fact, she had him wrapped around her little finger. All she had to do was look at Bob, give him that smile, and he would cave into her wants.*

*Not only were his grandchildren important to him, but Bob wanted to build a relationship with them. He enjoyed spending time with them just as God wants us to bond with Him.*

*According to scripture, a relationship with God is the best relationship we could ever have in this life. This was what Bob wanted to build with Matthew and Dana. He already had that relationship with their mother, Tami, and Bob was appreciative that Tami shared these precious children with him as well.*

*Bob's oldest son, Rob, lived in Guam .Bob often wished that Rob and family lived closer. Bob became so excited when they came for a visit one year. I remember the first time Bob got to see Reah. He couldn't get over how gorgeous she was with her olive complexion and beautiful eyes. What pleased him the most was that she wasn't afraid of him, as small children can sometimes be when they meet someone for the first time. He held her so proudly and carried her around. Robert John came along, and Bob felt flattered that they shared the same name and was pleased that his name would live on.*

*Would he one day be able to go fishing with Robert John? Bob would have wanted to spend time with his name sake, and would have taken the time to take him on his first fishing adventure. But, he also knew that his son, Rob, who is living in Guam, was a great fisherman. He could just imagine his son, Rob, with that little Robert John, fishing and taking in the beautiful sunsets on that little island of Guam, basking in the beauty that God created.*

*Fortunately, Bob did get to see and hold Robert John. but Bob passed away before he had the opportunity to take John Robert fishing and spend one-on-one with him.*

*I believe that Bob is in heaven fishing with Jesus. Even though Bob's youngest son, Daryl, didn't have children, Bob and Daryl did go fishing together. It was important to Bob that his relationship with his children would be a wonderful memory he could leave with them. Bob was the happiest when he was around people he loved. Daryl had a lot of his father's innate talents, and Bob was very proud of Daryl.*

*I just know when Daryl is sitting on the banks of a calm, blue, lake, he still envisions his father alongside him.*

*Every relationship that we've ever had, stemmed from God.*

*Our ultimate aim should be to have a relationship with God, just as Bob desired to have that time with his children and grandchildren.*

*When we think of the happiest time in our lives, what was it that brought us so much joy? It was probably spending time with the people we love. God created us with that in mind. God wants us to spend time with Him. He wants to know you and for you to know Him. He wants you to have that love for all eternity. Our knowledge of God is actually the best relationship we can ever have!*

*Grandpa Bob is in eternity, and I'd like to think that late at night, or early in the morning, that Rob, Tami, and Daryl know how much their earthly father loved them, and that they appreciate how much their Heavenly Father loves them. For Matthew, Dana, Robert John, Reah, and little Amila, I pray that you know how much you are loved by your family and by Jesus Christ himself. Relationships are important, and I can't think of anyone more important to have in your life than God, Himself.*

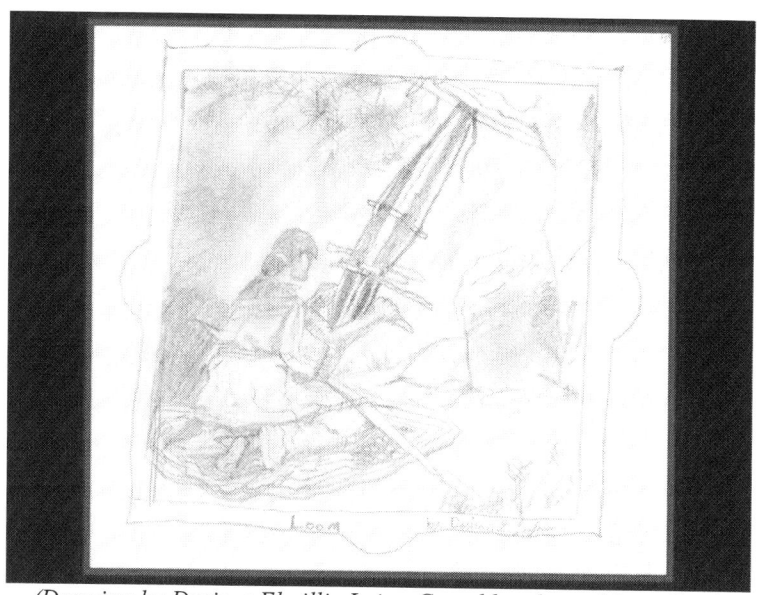

*(Drawing by Desirae Elmillie Lujan Granddaughter of Joan Koss)*

# *Day Thirty-Two*
## *The Master Weaver*

Moving to Sun City, Arizona brought Bob and me a lot of opportunities. Sun City is a resort town that has a wide variety of interests and activities. It is an adult community where a person can be as active as they wish. Of course, Bob and I decided to take the opportunity to be involved in other things besides playing golf.

My new adventure was learning to weave. Weaving was one of the most important and best developed of the crafts in Biblical times. Moses' real mother wove a reed basket for Moses when she put him in the Nile River.

Of course, a knowledge of the technique of weaving is necessary. First you have to learn the right terms used for the loom, and you have to learn to wrap your yarn and your weft yarn.

It took me more time to get the loom ready for weaving than it took to actually weave a tapestry.

Psalm 139 speaks of God as the "Weaver of Life." We belong to God. We are his handiwork. As the Weaver, God's involvement in life starts long before birth. Therefore he knows us, truly knows us, even our thoughts.
It was God who knit us together in our mother's womb, and it is God who is busy weaving us throughout the years, helping us to become what He desires us to be, His masterpiece.

God is the Weaver of our lives, and we are God's handiwork in progress, but we are not yet finished. God's desire is to make us into the kind of people He would have us to be. Each day brings a new possibility of adding to our already existing tapestry, bringing us closer to completion.

We have only the ability to see the tapestry of our lives from the back side. We see the loose strings, the mismatched tied off pieces, and the broken strands. God focuses on the ultimate finished piece, the front side, the beautiful design.

There are times when our lives look very bleak, and we wonder, "How can we be part of God's Tapestry"? There are times we look at ourselves, and we don't like our tapestry.

We don't like the hurt, pain, and disappointments, but we need to look at Psalms again and realize that God is the weaver . It is our responsibility to be open to what God's plan for us is.

We are God's work in progress.
God is the Weaver, and we are God's handiwork.
We need to allow the Holy Spirit to guide us, as we walk with God.

God is working on a masterpiece, and He has our best interest at heart.

*(The Loom - Drawing by Desirae Elmillie Lujan
Granddaughter of Joan Koss)*

*(Drawing by Desirae Elmillie Lujan Granddaughter of Joan Koss)*

## *Day Thirty-Three*
*Feelings of Loneliness*

*Even today, it pains me to remember back to a time when loneliness overpowered me.*

*I was a mother of three beautiful children, and the world was at my fingertips. But I had allowed another human being to tear down my self-esteem. I felt worthless and alone.*

*I was living in a situation in which I didn't feel anyone out there could understand what I was going through, not even God. I lost perspective on how big my problem was, and I was feeling sorry for myself.*

*I felt so empty inside, and so alone. When I hear about someone who is depressed, I hurt for them. I understand the hopelessness that they are feeling, and I often wish there was something that I could say to help relieve their pain. Although, I cannot help them, I can offer them a life jacket, and tell them to cling to the God who took away my pain and heartache. Jesus Christ Himself wants to intervene in their situation and in their life, just as He has done for me.*

*In the depths of my loneliness and depression, I felt no one would care if I were to die or even shed a tear over my grave. These feelings were so strong that one evening, I caved into my feelings and attempted suicide. I was rushed to the hospital and placed in the psychiatric unit.*

*A few months after my suicide attempt, I was released from the hospital. I was invited to go on a ski trip with a friend of mine, whose beauty and personality attracted everyone. The trip was good therapy for me. I had never laughed so hard in my life. It had been a long time since I remember laughing, just to be laughing.*

*The entire time, my friend kept saying, "Isn't this fun?" We were creating fun as we went. I guess I had always expected "fun" to fall out of the sky. I don't know, but for the first time I realized fun is what you make it. I began to realize that it was possible to have fun in spite of my circumstances.*

*I finally understand it. I had spent years in misery, isolating myself from others, clinging to pain, refusing to participate in life, because I was sad. I had played a part in my own misery, because I had failed to take the time to enjoy even the simple things in life.*

*Loneliness is a state of mind, an emotion brought on by feelings of being separated from other people. The worst part of all this was that I had been keeping friends at arm's length. In my sorrow and sadness, I had learned to retreat and hide away, isolating myself from friends. The more depressed I got, the more I hid away. The more I hid away, the lonelier I felt.*

*That trip taught me that I did have friends that were concerned about me. But more importantly, I discovered that the God of the universe cared about me, and yet in myself wallowing, I had shut Him out.*

*I have since learned that there is no situation so distressing or dangerous that God does not understand.*

*God's Spirit will give you the power to live like God wants you to live. The Holy Spirit guides, comforts, teaches, empowers, and produces within a Christian the actual characteristics of God, the fruit of the Spirit: love, joy, peace, patience, and more (Galatians 5:22-23).*

*The Bible says that Jesus "bore our grief's" on the cross (Isaiah 53:4 NAS). He feels our pain as strongly as we do, and will carry it for us. Give your hurt to Him. Then resolve not to dwell on it again. Take time to laugh with your family and friends, and leave the rest up to God.*

*When our spirits are overwhelmed by distress and filled with discouragement, all that we can see are the snares on every side. That is when we need to step out of our circumstances and embrace the promises of God and cling to His friendship. Isolation is often self-induced, but even those times in which it is not, God is always there waiting*

*to fellowship with us. God is real and we do not have to ever feel lonely.*
*Romans 8:35-39*

*$^{35}$Who shall separate us from the love of Christ? Shall tribulation, or distress, or persecution, or famine, or nakedness, or peril, or sword?*

*$^{36}$As it is written, for thy sake we are killed all the day long; we are accounted as sheep for the slaughter.*

*$^{37}$Nay, in all these things we are more than conquerors through Him who loved us.*

*$^{38}$For I am persuaded, that neither death, nor life, nor angels, nor principalities, nor powers, nor things present, nor things to come,*

*$^{39}$ nor height, nor depth, nor any other creature, shall be able to separate us from the love of God, which is in Christ Jesus our Lord.*

## Day Thirty-Four
### Homelessness

*When God begins opening doors for you in your life, he doesn't ask if this is what you want to do. He opens the door, and waits for you to take the step of obedience.*

*For years God opened up doors for me to get involved with various Prison ministries. BUT, THIS WAS NOT WHAT I WANTED TO DO, period, end of story.*

*After my son got out of prison, I didn't want to see another prison, or even drive by one. Yet, I could feel God nudging me. It seemed that I couldn't go anywhere that I didn't meet someone who had been in prison, or had a family member who was serving time.*

*It was then that my son, Darin, spoke wisdom into my heart and gently reminded me that if I didn't do what God was asking of me, I was in essence blocking all the blessings God had in store for me. I did want God's blessing, but I didn't want anything to do with prisons or prisoners. That is, until God reminded me of the story of Jonah. God had asked Jonah to go into Niveah, Jonah refused and wound up in the belly of a whale. Finally, God got his attention.*

*I was at work one day when I was approached by a mother whose daughter was in prison. Her plea tugged at my heart. I saw the hopelessness and desperation in her eyes. It was the same hopelessness that I had once felt.*

*All she wanted was for someone to reach out to the daughter. I wanted to say, no, but I couldn't. I mustered up all the emotional strength I could, and prayed as I drove up to the prison. It brought back a flood of memories. I had no idea if I could do it, but looking back, I'm so glad I did.*

*I had been visiting this young lady for several weeks when someone told me about an organization called, Kairos Outside a ministry dedicated to supporting the families of men or women who are, or have been incarcerated in the country's state or federal correctional facilities, as well as county jails or offender programs. The fact is that the ones who are incarcerated aren't the only ones doing time. Their families are doing time right along with them. Having a loved one in prison is often emotionally, financially and physically exhausting.*

*Again, I wasn't too interested but after being pressured, or what I felt was pressure, I agreed to attend one of their Kairos Outside weekends. That experience changed my life, and I didn't come home the same person. It was an amazing program, and I didn't want to leave.*

*I became involved in Kairos and felt this was my calling. I was getting in my comfort zone once again, when a woman who I had meet through Karios, asked me if I would like to come along with her and a few of her friends to feed the homeless in Arizona.*

*I was not interested, absolutely not! You see, I have always felt that these people are homeless for a reason. They have chosen to be there. They smell, they are dirty, and they are disgusting. No, thank you, this was a ministry that I wanted nothing to do with.*

*But, God had other plans. For three years, I went into down town Phoenix, Arizona to feed the homeless, not in a shelter, but out in a parking lot, right on the streets.*

*My job was to pick up bread and sweet rolls from a super market that furnished these items for us. I would fill my van up with goodies and take them to the parking lot where we greeted and fed the homeless. God was doing a work in my heart, he was changing me from the inside out.*

*There was a team there that sang Christian songs. We also had a minister who would preach, and our whole team would pray for and with the homeless. What an uplifting experience!*

*What an attitude change I had to go through. God had to show me that these people are His people, and He loves them equally, He loves them as much as He loved me. I got to know these people, and I listened to their personal stories, their heartaches, sometimes they even shared with me their dreams.*

*I discovered that although many of these individuals were on drugs, God was desperately trying to get through to them. He felt their pain; God loved them with all His heart. I met individuals who were living with mental illnesses, but some had just run into bad luck. I had the privilege of praying with them, providing them with food, and becoming their encourager. God was using me to bless His children.*

*I remember one day, when one of the men came into our little camp. He was obliviously demon possessed, and high on something. He demanded coffee, which we just ran out of, and instead, I offered him a sweet roll. This set him off into a rage, because he wanted coffee, not a sweet roll. He was angered and lifted his arm in an attempt to hit me. To my surprise many of the homeless people jumped to my defense ready to protect me. It was all I could do, but cry. I had spent years judging the homeless and yet, that night I discovered an invaluable lesson. These men and women had come to my defense when I needed help.*

*I've seen first-hand what compassion and prayer can do for a human being. Through my involvement with Kairos, I met a couple of friends who used to call the streets their home. I watched them change before my very own eyes. They responded to the love and now have a place of their own, and are willing to do anything for the kingdom of God. They both have been a blessing in my life. God continues to amaze me. If I hadn't of gone out of my comfort zone, I would of missed out on this blessing.*

*Going out on a limb and responding to God, has changed my attitude and my heart. Although, I still feel that many of those men and women, who are living on the streets, are there because of decisions they've made, I also know that some are out there who just need a helping hand to get them out of the circumstance. But more importantly, I now realize that God cares deeply for each of these individuals and his desire is that we comfort them and treat them like human beings.*

*In reading out of "The Message Bible"*

*Matthew 25: 35-36*
*"Then the King will say to those on his right, 'Enter, you who are blessed by my Father! Take what's coming to you in this kingdom. It's been ready for you since the world's foundation. And here's why:*
*I was hungry and you fed me,*
*I was thirsty and you gave me a drink,*
*I was homeless and you gave me a room,*
*I was shivering and you gave me clothes,*
*I was sick and you stopped to visit,*
*I was in prison and you came to me.'*

*Did I ever expect to be involved with the homeless or prisoners? NO, but God had different plans for me. I am no longer involved in feeding the homeless, but God has opened another door for me in the prison ministry, with a group called, Daughters of Destiny. I'm just waiting for the prison to badge me so I can go inside the prison to do Bible studies for the women here in Arizona.*

*I keep thinking I'm getting too old for God to use me, but I guess that is what Sarah thought too. Serving God is such an amazing journey. I can't wait to see what else He has in store for me. What is God calling you to do? Maybe it's time I pass down the wisdom that my son gave to me, "If you aren't obedient to the gentle nudges of God in your life, then you miss out on the blessings." So, what are you waiting for? Step out in faith and ask God to lead you.*

## *Day Thirty-Five*
### *Women of Strength, Women of Valor*

*God has an important calling for older women. The book of Titus tells us that the older women shall take the younger women under their wings to teach them how to live the Christian life.*

*I was blessed to have a mother who loved God. Mom understood how important the scriptures were and how important prayer was. I was raise by a mother who spent her spare time on her knees in prayer. She prayed on behalf of her family, her neighbors, and her community. It was Mom's desire that all her children come to know God.*

*I didn't lack for role models. My paternal grandma, whom I called Mutta, was a special part of my life growing up, and that I will always cherish. Mutta spent quality time with me. She sang to me, taught me prayers, and brought a whole new dimension to a relationship between a grandmother and granddaughter.*

*I used to love to climb in bed with her as a child and talk with her before crawling back to my bed. She would recite prayers with me that were so unique and easy to understand. One of those prayers made me feel especially safe at night. It was a prayer to God asking Him to send fourteen angels, two at the head, two at the feet, two on left side, two on the right side, two to cover me, two to wake me, and two to take me to heaven if I died.*

*Mutta was born in Teplitz, Bessarabia in South Russia. She was an orphan and alone until she met my grandfather and married. Times were tough, and when her sons got older, the family decided to flee to the United States.*

*Their plan was for my grandfather to take half of the kids to America, and then later, my Mutta would bring the other children to America. However, Mutta was stopped at the border, and sent back. My father was one of the children who had to remain behind with his mother. Since my father was sick at the time, he was not allowed to board the ship, therefore my grandma decided to stay behind.*

*I often marvel at the strength of this woman. She had no idea if she'd ever see her husband and older children ever again. Her faith was the only thing that kept her going. Her God was all she had to rely on at this point in time. It took six months before she was able to get to America to be reunited with her husband and children. Mutta finally had to hide my father amongst the baggage so that he could make the passage with the family.*

*Many families were forced to sell their children in order to afford the passage over to America. The reign of Queen Victoria at that time was ruthless, and families were desperate to flee to America. How difficult and heartbreaking for those people who resorted to that choice for their lives.*

*Grandmother was a Titus woman. She was strong, compassionate, and she passed down her faith to her grandchildren. Mutta became what was known as "The Settlement Doctor", and delivered her last baby, her great granddaughter, at the age of 79. She knew her time as a doctor had ended due to her dimming eyesight. The lives this woman touched with her faith and her healing hands are numerous. She is unforgettable by all who are left to remember her.*

*Mutta didn't speak English. She spoke in her native tongue, which was a \*dialect mixed with a little bit of Russian. I didn't learn English until I started school. In our community, it was frowned upon to speak anything other than English out in public. I eventually stopped speaking my native language altogether once my grandmother died. Looking back, I regret that I didn't keep it up, but I let peer pressure and the fear of Hitler's reign, take that gift from me.*

*My memories of my grandma have faded, except I can still feel the love this woman showed me. These memories will live in my heart forever. There was a special bond of friendship between a granddaughter and a grandmother. I now work in a health care center, and I have gotten attached to many of these women. Even though some of them have memory problems, they still seem to be there to give me inspiration and joy. Most of them do not understand why God hasn't taken them home. I feel He still has work for them to do on earth. One of those jobs is to inspire younger women.*

*It has saddened me, at times, to watch as these courageous women lose their ability to walk, and are confined to a nursing home, isolated from their former lives. Yet, God has shown me that these women still have a special gift to share. Just as Titus tells us, the older women are there to guide us with our Christian walk, these women have the ability and life experience to impart wisdom, if we would only listen.*

*The older woman has been down the road that these younger woman are about to embark upon.*

*Proverbs 31:10-31 shares with us what a virtuous woman's view is on what it takes to be a worthy woman. We learn to value such wisdom in our lives, and teach our daughters that wisdom in their lives. Women of this kind of virtue are, "very precious in the sight of God."*

*There is so much to be learned from our mothers, our aunts, and our grandmothers. I pray that God raises up a generation of older women who see the light in the passage of Titus 2.*

*What an incredible calling! As a woman, I pray that we can each reach up and seek the advice and wisdom from those who have gone before us; that we can gently guide and encourage those women who are younger than we are. The beauty and the strength of womanhood can be found in a Titus Woman.*

*NOTE:*
*\* Many of the Black Sea Germans from Russia originally came from the South or Southwest areas of Germany so they spoke one of the many High German dialects. They did not speak Low German or Platt Deutsch. The one group of people who did speak Low German is the Mennonites who originally came from northern Germany. Our Germans from Russia dialects are older than the language in present day Germany*

*http://lib.ndsu.nodak.edu/grhc/articles/newspapers/news/dialect.html*
*Michael.Miller@ndsu.edu*

## *Day Thirty-Six*
## *The Tale of Two Women*

*This is a tale of two women, born on opposite sides of the track.*

*I'm one of these women.*
*The one, is a city girl raising two small children, who is young, full of life, and loves her children.*

*The other women, is a farmer's daughter, who has three grown children whom she adores.*

*The difference of ages between the two women is about 40 years.*

*The younger city woman, was full of spirit, loved her friends, but the night life of drugs consumed her, and she made no time for God.*

*As life would have it, this woman met hurt, heartache, and rejection.*

*She learned to cover her conscience and pain with drugs. Her lifestyle finally caught up with her, and this beautiful, dark haired, young girl wound up in prison.*
*With tears in her eyes and hand cuffs on each wrist, she cried out softly,*
*"God, I can't face another day. I am ready to end it all."*
*At this point, she could no longer see hope, and was facing a sentence behind bars for the second time.*

*"My children won't need me. I'm depressed and hurt. I'm not sure I want to go on." She was ready to end it all, and was placed under a suicide watch in prison.*
*God heard this young girl's cries. God knew this woman, and He knew how she felt.*

**Let's take a moment and go to the farmer's daughter.**
*This older woman was born and raised in a country church, but as she got older, she too, grew up wanting all that this world had to offer.*

*She had always held good jobs, brought her family up in church, and her friends thought this woman had it altogether.*

*She was actually quite good at concealing the pain and hurt that life had thrown her way.*

*But she was hurting inside, and after years of pain and heartache, she attempted suicide.*

*She was committed to a psych hospital, where she pleaded with God to come to her aid.*

*Eventually, this woman ended up stepping through the heavy doors of a prison waiting room.*

*As she held her shoulders high, she prayed under her breath "Lord, I cannot keep entering through these prison doors much longer. I am embarrassed, hurt ,and I feel helpless."*

*Prison was no place for either of the two women. Neither one wanted to be behind bars, as an inmate or even as a visitor.*

*The loud clang of the prison doors opened, and the farmer's daughter greeted her son as he walked through the door in his prison garb.*

*Her son was a man clothed in false pride, a scar across his cheek, and a tear falling down his face. A tear faded as quickly as it had dropped. He found comfort that his mother had come for yet another visit.*

*This woman visited a son whom she loved. This was her son she had high hopes for, and for whom she had prayed for only the best.*

*She hid her pain well, and the only one who really knew how she felt was God. To gain her strength and to move forward, she cried out to God for her son.*

*But, would her prayers mean anything thing to God?
The future looked bleak, but she loved her son, so she
continued to pray.*

*Her prayers were answered.*

*After being released from prison, and years later, God
broke through to her son. He got saved, and eventually
went on to become a pastor of a church.*

**Now, if you can, I want to quickly go back to the first
woman in my story, the one in prison.**
*This young woman was ready to end it all.
She wanted to kill herself.*

*She didn't know God, but God knew her.
God brought the farmer's daughter into her life. The
farmer's daughter knew what it was like to have a child
behind bars. When she learned about this broken hearted
city girl from the girl's mother, she rose to the occasion and
offered to pray for her and to make a visit to prison to tell
the young woman about the Lord, to bring her hope.*

*When the two women meet, it was friendly, but the visit was
intense and emotional.*

*Unbeknownst to this farmer's daughter, this young gal in
prison, was ready to kill herself, and was prepared to
do it at any time.*

*God had sent the farmer's daughter to confront the young
girl.*

*Two women from opposite sides of the track had something
in common.*

*They both had embraced the pains of this world. Both wanted to end their lives.*

*This was a divine appointment.
The miracle of this story is that
I am the farmer's daughter who had the wonderful opportunity to bring hope to this young woman in prison.*

*If it had not been for my son having served a prison sentence for manslaughter and seeing how God transformed his life in prison because of prayer, then, I would have not had the opportunity to walk through those prison doors and meet with the younger woman, that day, to give her the hope of God's freedom that she was searching for.*

*This young woman has been transforming right before my eyes, and I see God, too, working in her life. Who knows what God has in store for this young, free spirited, woman? I can still remember the shame of having to wait my turn in the prison waiting room to visit with my son, and yet I had no choice.*

*I was his mother, and I was not going to give the devil authority over his life.*

*But with this younger woman, I have a choice.
Even though it is painful, and brings back the horrible memories of visiting my son in prison, it also brought back the memories I felt being locked up in the mental hospital. I, too, was behind bars, locked up with no freedom, mentally or physically. I feel God is using me to touch her life, to give her hope that He can and does change people.*

*These two women share so much in common,
a love for their children, a family who loves them, and both
live in a real world full of commotion and chaos.
The city girl meets Christ behind a prison door in the midst
of hardship.*

*The farmer's daughter meets Him in a little old country
church.*

*The city girl has yet to see the wonderful plans God has for
her and her children.*

*The farmer's daughter has seen and continues to see God
moving in her life and in her children's lives.*

*The moral of this story could be many things, but I know
that God does turn disappointments to victory. With God,
the devil is defeated.*

*This young girl in prison needs our prayers for
encouragement.*

*God is what this story is all about. He had a unique
purpose for my life, for my children's lives, and for this
young woman in prison.*

*He has a unique purpose for everyone individually. God is
in the business of turning failures around.
He is an amazing God, and through him, all things are
possible.*

*Wall of bricks labeled: Alone, Shame, Angry, Lonely, Disappointment, Embarrassed, Helpless, Fear, Hurt, Rejection, Rejection, Panic, Self-Pity, Betrayed, Abandoned, Hatred, Guilt, Frustration, Abused, Hurt, Devastated, Anger, Guilt, Resentment, Bitterness*

## Day Thirty-Seven
## The Wall I Built Brick by Brick

*In my life I had built up a very high, thick wall. For a while, that wall felt so comfortable, but over time I began to feel pretty lonely behind this wall. Eventually, this wall began to feel more like a prison wall and a barrier in my life.*

*At first it felt good to feel that bitterness, hate, and anger, but I was becoming a very miserable person.*
*The building of my wall was a very slow process, but it eventually became a very sturdy wall. This was a wall that began as an emotional protection and wound up becoming a stifling obstruction in my life.*

*I had hidden myself behind that big thick wall for so long, I hadn't realized how isolated I had become. This wall blocked me from my friends and from my family. I was beginning to feel rejected and abandoned by all.*
*I even felt as if God had abandoned me. I hadn't realized, but I had actually built a wall that was blocking me from the presence of God.*

*Hidden in my self-pity and anger, my prayers did not seem to be getting through to God.*

*God didn't seem to be hearing my prayers, but I wasn't allowing God to speak to me either. I was refusing to bow in His presence. I was refusing to read His word, and I was refusing to seek His advice. Instead, I was telling God how I wanted my life to be.*

*In my case, it took over 20 some years for me to be able to tear down this wall that I had built over time.*
*I grew up in a Christian home, lived a very sheltered life, married young, and had three beautiful children. Things appeared to be going great in my life, until the devil started attacking my family.*

*I felt I had failed as a mother. Feeling like a failure led me to begin building that wall, and my first brick was failure.*

*Living with an abusive alcoholic caused my self-esteem to go down. Then the anger, frustration, and panic crept in when my husband decided to divorce me. I took this second brick called insecurity and cemented it up against that first brick.*

*It just seemed that things were getting worse, not better.*

*With each heartache and pain, I managed to cement in another brick to this wall. Eventually this wall grew so high, people couldn't look over it to see how much I was really hurting on the inside. Since I hadn't been outside of my wall for so long, I didn't feel I had anyone that I could turn to. I thought if this is how the rest of my life would be like, I didn't want to be here. My spirit was broken, so I attempted suicide.*

*I felt I had been betrayed and abandoned. I felt so helpless. This selfish act of mine caused hurt and disappointment to my children.*

*Suicide was not the answer. I needed to learn to deal with all my hurts and disappointments. I needed to turn them over to God.*

*I had to learn to forgive, and it started with a decision of wanting to be freed of my bitterness, hurt, and disappointment, that was blocking God's blessings from my life.*

*The first step in tearing down my wall, was to rid all the heartache and pain that I had harbored inside of me.*

*I needed to go to God in prayer, ask Him to relieve me of all that was troubling me on the inside, and to focus on God's love and grace.*

*When I was able to forgive the people who wronged me, God gave me a change of memory, and a change in my heart. It was then that my wall came down, and I was healed. I received my gift of forgiveness from God and became a new person.*

## *Day Thirty-Eight*
## *Our Miracle Grandbaby*

*The news of a new baby is always exciting. We await with eagerness and anticipation the arrival of that new bundle who will bring joy into our lives.*

*The day that my granddaughter arrived was even more special since it was a home delivery with a midwife. The whole family could be involved with this baby's birth. However, the timing wasn't good, as the main water line broke in front of the house. But my granddaughter decided she wasn't going to wait, water main problems or not. This was how Tanisha entered the world, overcoming all odds.*

*After a few months passed and this precious baby was not growing as she should, doctors told us that Tanisha had a metabolic defect. She was missing a very important enzyme vital to living, and the doctor's prognosis wasn't good.*

*We were told that this little girl, wouldn't be able to walk or sit up. She'd eventually have brain damage, and she couldn't live beyond a few short years without these enzymes. At the time, this was new territory in the medical world, and doctors did not have a solution.*

*Prayers were sent out all over, and our God came to her aid.*

*While she was supposed to be getting worse, she began improving day by day. Once more, she overcame the odds. God had other plans for her in life, and our prayers that were sent to our Heavenly Father stopped the devil in his tracks.*

*Today this same baby is a grown woman, with children of her own. She has been a blessing to others, especially to my sister who is suffering from Alzheimer's. She visits her on a regular basis, and even takes her to her Bible study group. God is using her. She is a strong believer, and credits God for saving her life. She believes in prayer, and has an anointing over her life. She is anxious to see what more God will do in her life.*
*Psalm 103:2-5*

*Bless the LORD, O my soul, and forget not all His benefits: Who forgives all your iniquities, Who heals all your diseases. Who redeems your life from destruction, Who crowns you with loving kindness and tender mercies, Who satisfies your mouth with good things, So that your youth is renewed like the eagles.*
*My husband, Bob, called her "Our Miracle Grandbaby!"*

*Psalm 34:15*
*The eyes of the LORD are upon the righteous, and his ears are open unto their cry.*

*(left Joan Koss right Marvie Kothman)*

## Day Thirty-Nine
*Respect*

*This page is dedicated to my niece, Marvie. Growing up, my niece was only four years younger than I, but at a young age, I felt that I was the superior one. Of course, at the age of seven, I was older, and I deserved the respect. I informed her that she had to call me "Aunt Joan" whether it be on school grounds or at home.*

*This has always been the topic at our family gatherings as it made for a good laugh. As I look back, I wonder if I give God the same respect that I expected from my niece. I knew she loved me, but I wanted that title, and respect "AUNT."*

*Our very first commandment is in Exodus 20:2 KJV "Thou shall have no other Gods before me." We love God, but do we respect him? Do we bow before God?*

*David was a man of God, who tried doing things that were pleasing to God, but when he messed up, he repented quickly. He respected who God was.*

*I truly want to respect God, but in my busy day, I sometimes forget that I need God. I often find myself making decisions, without ever consulting God.*

*If I truly respect God for who He is, I would want to include him in ALL aspects of my life.*

*My niece and I are both adults, living our own lives, but even today, she gives me the respect that I asked for as a little girl.*

*Marvie has always been there to give me support when I needed it. Even though she recently has been diagnosed with muscular dystrophy, and has an eye condition that has pretty much left her blind in one eye, she is still there for me.*

*She has put the final touches on this devotion book for me, and for this, I'm truly grateful that she cared and RESPECTED me enough to want the best for me. I value her friendship.*

*May we all become men and women who are respecters of God, not because we have to, but because we want to. God is the King of Kings, the Lord of Lords, and the God of Gods. It is an honor to be called his children.*

*(Painting by Joan's grandaughter - Darleen L.Tankersley)*

## *Day Forty*
*The Number 40*

*The number 40 in the Bible is symbolic of a "PERIOD OF TESTING."*

*Every time forty (days, weeks, years) is mentioned in the Bible, it is always in reference to a period of testing and probation. Each of these periods end ultimately with a blessing.*

*Just as Noah's faith was put to the test with 40 days and nights of rain; the Children of Israel were tested in the wilderness for 40 years.*

*God allowed Goliath to taunt Israel for 40 days, and Jesus fasted 40 days before he began his public ministry.*

*By the time I had reached the age of 40, I had gone through a lot of tragedy, years of agonizing hurts and wounds. The devil tried to destroy all three of my children, thankfully he didn't prevail, but he did put stumbling blocks in my path to help ruin my marriage.*

*Little by little, I came to a realization that the sooner I get to Jesus, the sooner He's able to heal me. This is what Jesus does. He is our Shepherd.*

*He will rescue us and pull us out of the ravine. He'll hook his staff around us and pull us out of the place where we couldn't rescue ourselves.*

*The Shepherd will do something else if we continually look to provide for ourselves, heal ourselves, and blame others for our pain. Eventually the Shepherd will get his sheep (us). He'll hold His sheep down, get His rod, and lay it over the leg of the sheep, and press with His knee until He breaks the leg. Then He will carry the sheep on His shoulders, until the sheep is healed.*

*A shepherd who is gracious will break a sheep's leg to save the sheep's life. Once the sheep is healed, it will never leave the Shepherd's side.*

*We know that whatever hurts come our way, our Lord and Savior, our Shepherd, will quickly heal us.*

*This was what God had to do with me when things in my life were going awry. I was locked in a mental hospital, because I tried killing myself. God allowed this to happen. There have been a few times in my life that God has had to break my leg so to speak, to save my life.*

*Trying to do everything in my own power. I wasn't relying on His strength. It was then I realized that I needed God, and He would be the only one who could rescue me.*

*God restored my hope and painted in my life a brighter future. He blessed me with a new husband, and restored my soul.*

*Through my husband, God show me how to laugh, have fun, and walk in God's path.*

*Now I can see the end results, of what was happening in my life. Knowing the end, and looking back at the struggles I went through, God was by my side the whole time. I just didn't realize it.*

*Today it's like reviewing a movie, knowing that God is going to win. So why did I let fear grip me and wear me out to the extent that I tried taking my own life? It is all in knowing that the devil was not going to destroy my children. God used all their of their tragedies in life, and He is using my children for His Glory. God is still sitting on the throne in Heaven. He is the same God today, yesterday, as He will be the same God tomorrow too.*

*I'm not trying to say that trial and tribulations will not come my way, but I know that God will be there for me.*

*Where are you in your journey? If you are in the depth of your sorrows, you may be in the "40" days, in the testing period. Let God comfort you. He wants to heal you. He wants to provide for you. But you do need to come to Him.*

*Joan is an author, public speaker, who says, "God is good and his mercy endures forever."*

## *"Bowing Before God" a woman's devotional, a must read, written by Joan M. Koss*

*This book is not to be used in place of a Bible, but as a morning devotional to add to your spiritual walk.*

*"I owe so much to Christ for all he has done in my life, and a special thanks to God for waking me in the wee hours of the morning bringing to my remembrance my life story for this book. I pray that this book touches your life, and that God revels Himself to you. "Amen.*

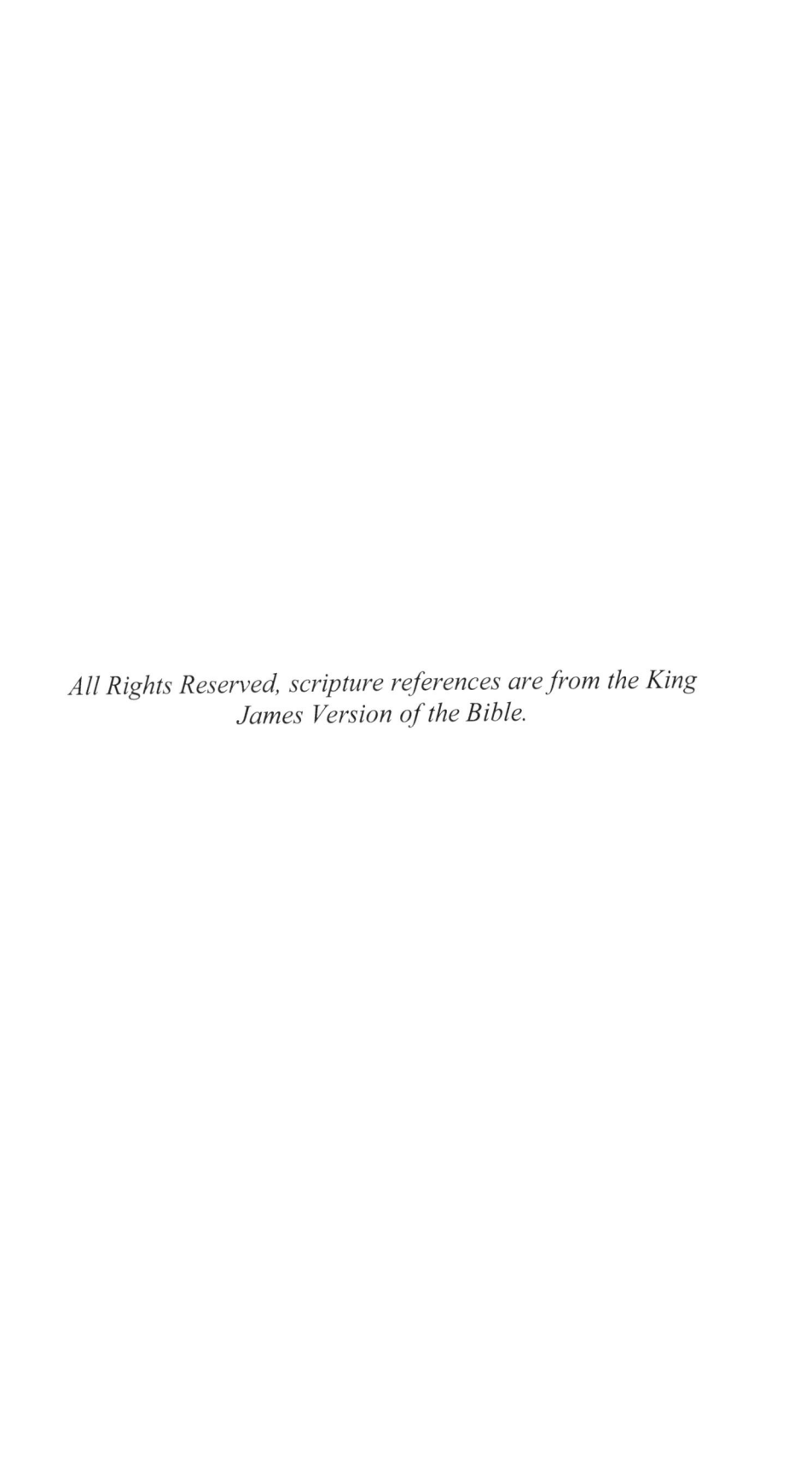

*All Rights Reserved, scripture references are from the King James Version of the Bible.*

*Thank you Jesus, for the time that I had with Robert Koss, my husband, friend, and soul mate.*

***Co-Author of "Bowing Before God", is Joan's oldest daughter, Teila (Carroll) Tankersley.***

*Teila has authored and co-authored several books which include:*

- *Harrison High School Pioneers & Alumni, by Teila Tankersley*
- *Torn/Apart Restored written by Darin Carroll and co-authored by Teila Tankersley*
- *A Heart Held Ransomed written by Steve Stotko and co-authored by Teila Tankersley*

*She writes on topics and subjects that are inspirational and have the potential to change lives. There's more to this life than just living and dying.*

Made in the USA
Lexington, KY
15 September 2011